A Little Dutch Maiden V2: A South African Sketch

Harriet Ella Ernle Money

A LITTLE DUTCH MAIDEN.

𝔄 𝔖𝔬𝔲𝔱𝔥 𝔄𝔣𝔯𝔦𝔠𝔞𝔫 𝔖𝔨𝔢𝔱𝔠𝔥.

BY

E. ERULE MONEY.

IN TWO VOLUMES.
VOL. II.

LONDON:

RICHARD BENTLEY AND SON,

Publishers in Ordinary to Her Majesty the Queen.

1887.

256

A LITTLE DUTCH MAIDEN.

CONTENTS OF VOL. II.

A LITTLE DUTCH MAIDEN.

CHAPTER I.

OF A 'SMOUSER' AND A BUNCH OF ROSES.

 WEEK had gone by. A week is so long, or so short—so much in our lives, or again nothing. So little a space for rejoicing—such length of days to suffer in.

Things at Craigmount were looking well ; heavy rains had broken up the drought, and the weather was cold again. Mr. Craig had returned from his journey, bringing the breezy cheeriness into the house that usually attended his advent. Jack went about as usual, and if his heart ached, it made little outward difference in him. He was a little graver and sterner than his wont, perhaps, kept a little more to himself; his face was paler, his eyes had darker circles under them, and his laugh seemed to have lost its mirth; but since Dollie had spoken the word which severed their lives, Jack had never been heard by anyone to allude to the affair. The exciting events of the night, which the others had almost forgotten, had been amply discussed by them at the time. Two or three indifferent Dutchmen had dropped in the next day and commented upon the matter to their English acquaintances with an expressive shrug of the shoulders.

'Max was in liquor? Yes, no doubt; but he meant what he said all the same— they had heard him say so before. Why did the girl go on fooling him if she did not want him? Her father? Ah, yes;

Jan had his reasons, no doubt. Well, she had done the best thing at last, else she would probably have lost them both. Not but what Dollie Haardman could have had her pick—she was the beauty of the valley, etc. 'Twas a pity the Englishman was so taken up with her that he wanted to get shot ; ah, the mischief women did !'

The Englishmen considered it a 'd——d shame,' though they were not unanimous in fixing the blame ; and so they talked it over whenever Jack's back was turned, until the subject was worn out and dismissed.

In country life in South Africa, where topics are few, a new one is a boon ; but it is soon exhausted, because each one flings his or herself upon it with a rush and a clamour. It graces every meal, lurks in each teacup, and all tobacco-pouches, until sucked dry like a worn-out orange it is cast away, and the man's taste would be equally called in question that resuscitated either.

On this afternoon, at Craigmount, they were expecting their circle to be augmented by the arrival of Miss Wynyard and the Dares. The place was wearing holiday garb in honour of the occasion; there had been a great deal of sweeping of the stoop and the drive, of tying up climbers and refilling vases, and everyone looked a little anxious. In the confined life where people are so much dependent on each other for amusement and companionship, the question as to whether a new-comer will add to the conviviality or detract from it is an important one.

'Will she be jolly, or beastly nasty?' wondered Freddy inwardly, as he sat on the veranda with Robin and Seymour. 'Stuck up, *in course,* coming to a farm from the town, and fancying herself half-bred English.'

'I wonder,' he said aloud to Robin, as Seymour went in at the side-door, 'what's up with that fellow? In and out, like a cat on hot bricks! Now, if you were took like that, considerin'——'

'I am too old,' replied Robin. 'I have gone through all those hot and cold stages, and settled down into the placidity of middle life. Well, Seymour, have you found a pipe to suit you at last?'

'Given it up; got a book from Jack. He was reading it upside down, so I did not think it was of much use to him.'

'Jack, by-the-bye, seems to take life pretty easy, and I am glad to see it. Care killed a cat,' said Robin.

> ' " If she be not fair to me,
>   What care I how fair she be !" '

hummed Seymour.

'Those are your opinions, are they?' said Freddy scornfully. 'Well, if either of you want to change them, come and take my room for a night. I am pretty well tired of it.'

'How?'

' Because I never get a night's rest. Tramp, tramp, tramp, half the night. The petition's thin, you know, and it makes my head spin. It is enough to make a fellow see his grandmother's ghost.'

' Tap to him,' suggested Seymour.

' Oh no; I'll bear it while I can. Perhaps, if he couldn't walk it off, it would turn to suicide, or he'd murder me to relieve his feelings. But if he don't drop it soon after she's married, I shall become a raving lunatic.'

' More likely to walk *all* night then. Isn't it " Ouida " who says a man should be grateful to the woman that makes him miserable for a while by refusing him, instead of wretched for life by accepting him ?'

' " Ouida " has said a lot of darned rot,' growled Freddy. ' But there is commonsense in that.'

' She said that a pipe was a pocket philosopher; I swore by her for a whole day after I read that,' remarked Robin, fingering affectionately his shabby, travelled, brown pipe, with the names of most countries and towns on the globe roughly initialled on it. 'I fancy I hear the cart,' he said suddenly.

'I hope your hair is curled, and you have got the right scent on your handkerchief,' suggested Freddy.

'It would be proper in you to go and see,' said Seymour. 'Just stroll to the corner of the road, you may be—er—disappointed. There is always a glorious uncertainty about who will or won't come from that station.'

'There is no dust now, but that is the cart, sure enough,' said Freddy.

Jack came out on the stoop with a whip and yelled to the dogs, who were preparing for their usual rush.

'Strangers must think we are a set of lunatics, keeping such a pack of fools,' he said.

Having laid about him to his satisfaction,

he stood with the others watching the approach of the cart, shading his eyes with his hand. ' She is there,' he announced.

As it came round the corner Robin got up, and went down the steps to meet it.

' Now, then, behold Adair on duty !' said Freddy. ' He is going to pretend he is mortal eager to see her. See him twisting his face into an anxious expression——'

' Hush, you young vermin, before I throttle you !' commented Seymour pleasantly.

' Handsome girl,' said Jack shortly.

' If she looks handsome after a twelve-mile drive in a Cape cart, it is a—er—credit to her,' said Seymour.

Robin, with his cap in his hand, was standing by the cart where Mrs. Craig and Miss Wynyard were seated, his handsome head bowed courteously down to his *fiancée*, and his tongue running brightly and pleasantly as he took charge of their wraps.

' I thought you would have come to the

station,' said Miss Wynyard coldly, as she
gave him her hand to help her down.

'I should, certainly, but I feared you
might be crowded.'

'Crowded!' exclaimed Jack impatiently,
catching the words on the veranda. 'Why
didn't he ask me for a horse, then? When
a fellow has got a tongue in his head,
I can't be expected to think of everything.'

'Pure modesty, I should fancy,' said
Seymour, with a grin.

'I suppose I must go and say "How
do,"' remarked Jack, with a sigh. 'I
wonder how the mother likes her.'

He went up to her as she reached the
stoop, and Robin introduced him.

Miss Wynyard, who was a magnificent-
looking brunette, with dark hair and eyes,
clear white skin, and unusually brilliant
scarlet lips, looked him 'over,' Jack felt
with indignation.

Seeing that he was well-looking, and

not put out by her survey, she accorded him a more gracious bow than she had apparently at first intended.

'I hope you are not tired with the long drive,' he said.

'No, thank you, not at all.'

'I trust we shall be able to make your visit pleasant ; that you will not be dull here,' Jack added courteously, as he walked by her side into the house.

'You are very kind. One must be dull sometimes in this world ; it is unavoidable, and nothing to complain of.'

'She scores one,' thought Jack. 'I suppose she twigged I did not like her, and don't care a brass farthing whether she is dull or not.'

'I am sure you won't be dull,' said Robin, as he placed her shawls on the table. 'You will like the life very much when you get used to it. There is so much that is novel, and it is so——'

'What ?'

'I was going to say free-and-easy, but that hardly explains my meaning.'

'No? Oh, I don't intend to be dull.'

'I would not be Adair for many a thousand pound. A handsome devil !' commented Jack to himself as he went out on the stoop. 'Well, my friend, what is your pleasure?'

This was addressed to a 'smouser' who, pack on his back, had just arrived, and was panting, and preparing to unstrap himself.

'Nicsh thingsh,' he said, 'very nicsh thingsh, vat I bring. Cheap and good. Jewellery, thimbles, shilver buttons——'

'You had better go round to the back—don't make a mess here.'

'Will you want thingsh ? Will you buy?'

'No, I am sure we shan't. There has been one of you fellows here every day this week.'

The smouser's face fell.

'We vill see, we vill see. There is not

many mensch travel this line with thingsh like mine. Will I have some food there?'

' Oh, I suppose so.'

' Can you give me a bed?'

' No; you had better go on to the next farm.'

' How far is that?'

' Oh, not far,' said Jack brightly; 'just across the river. Mr. Dare's or Mr. Helmsley's.'

' Ah. How long will I be getting there?'

' Bother! How should I know? Depends on how you walk.'

' Will you say it is an hour?'

' I will say nothing—except, clear out of this! Take your wares round.'

' Last night,' said the smouser reflectively, ' I slept by Mynheer Haardman. Gave me goot bed, not close, not so Dutch —bought a lot of thingsh. Young lady going to be married. Bought a nicsh chain —de debbel, dat was a nice goot chain—dat weigh heavy! Let her have it cheap, coos

it was for the young man. I have got
another of them, dirt cheap—shall I show
it to you, sir ?'

'No!' thundered Jack, turning away.

'Jack, what has the man got ?' asked
Mrs. Craig, looking out of the door. 'I
wanted——'

'Everything, madam,' returned the
smouser, with a sweeping bow.

'I have mislaid one of my thimbles, and
you know I always like to keep two. Have
you got any thimbles ?'

'Yesch, all thimbles ; little, big—little
money, musch money — but all goot.'
And with a flourish the smouser spread out
a tray, talking volubly the while.

'Do come and tell me if these thimbles
are silver, dear,' said Mrs. Craig, pursuing
Jack up the stoop. 'You know these men
will say anything.'

Unwillingly enough Jack returned.

The thimble was selected, and as he was
turning it round in his fingers, a locket and

chain in the tray caught his eye. He started, and the thimble rolled away upon the stoop.

'Confound it!' said Jack hoarsely.

'Never mind, dear, I will find it;' and Mrs. Craig pursued the thimble on its way.

'How did you come by that?' said Jack in a low tone, pointing to the locket.

'Ah, ah—dat is second-hand.'

'Speak! or I will wring your neck——'

'Here it is, dear,' said Mrs. Craig triumphantly. 'The cock picked it up, but I was too quick for him.'

'It is a good one, mother. Come to my room when you have done,' added Jack to the smouser. 'Perhaps, after all, I may find you have something I want.'

Leaning in the doorway of his room, Jack waited.

'Now,' he said, as the smouser at length came up to him, 'no beating about the bush. Where did you get that locket and chain?'

The man looked up, and, apparently

assured that Jack was not in a mood to be
trifled with, replied :

'From the young lady at the Dutch farm
—Haardman's.'

'Do you mean she sold it to you ?' Jack
knocked out each syllable with difficulty.

'Eh? She parted with it—yesch. How
else should I have it ?'

With a smothered exclamation, Jack took
a turn in the room.

'Now,' he said, stopping in front of the
man suddenly, 'if you are lying it shall go
hard with you. Why did she part with
it ?'

'Why? I suppose because her father, or
her husband that is to be, would not let her
keep it, and—she wanted many thingsh.
But it is gold, goot gold, and heavy,' said
the man, returning to his former manner.

'Why do you tell me it is gold ?' asked
Jack scornfully. 'Do you think I am ass
enough to buy it ?'

'I thought the shentlemans seemed to

take a kind of fancy to it, and the young lady was desirous you should have it.'

' That I should have it !' said Jack with astonishment, but an eager look in his face.

' Yesch, if you did not mind its being second-hand. But, really, it is as good as new.'

' Well, what do you want for it ?' asked Jack, looking at him with a sudden change of manner.

' Ah, dear! it is second-hand, but I dare say it cost ten when it was new.'

' No, it cost five,' said Jack quietly.

' Ah, dear! the shentlemans must have seen it before, or one like it. Vell, shall we say five ? I must not lose by it.'

' Rot !' said Jack, looking at him steadily and putting down three sovereigns on the table. ' There is my bid, and the only one.'

The smouser took them up and bit them attentively ; then he slipped them into his pocket, and handed the locket and chain to Jack.

'Now,' said Jack, 'that you have that money safe, perhaps you will tell me the truth. Why did she part with this?'

'I did tell you the truth, my goot shentlemans. She said—let me think—that she had always worn it, but now in the time coming she could not; she was afraid the father or the young man would destroy it if they saw it again, and she had nowhere really safe to put it by. So she thought she would rather you had it, and you was, she hoped, to think much of it; of course, being goot gold, you would.'

'One more question,' said Jack. 'What did she sell it to you for?'

'I did not say she sell it, I say she parted with it—which is true. I was quite willing to buy it; I offered her a better chain of mine for it, but she would not take it. Ah, the foolish woman!'

'You rascal!' exclaimed Jack; 'I should like to run you up to the top of the flagstaff with my own hands.'

'My dear shentlemans,' said the Jew, bowing himself out of the door, 'if you will make de mistake it is not my fault. And, see, I cannot carry wares about the country for nosching whatever!'

Jack, left alone, opened the locket. On one side was his own photo — that had always been there—but on the other side was something new—a likeness of Dollie, lifelike, and one little curl of golden hair.

'Poor little Dollie—poor, dear little love!' said Jack with deep tenderness, as he sat upon his bed and gazed on it. 'She has not forgotten, then.'

Jack did not kiss his locket, and did not cry over it; but he felt as if he might be within an ace of doing both, so he got down and locked it away in a drawer.

*   *   *   *   *   *

Rockingham Dare was tooling his cart along merrily, bringing it up to the stoop in a style that showed to advantage his four horses, who were marvels in matching and breed for that neighbourhood.

Mr. Craig and Mr. More, who had also returned from their drive, were standing on the veranda watching him.

'Heigh-ho, Dare! can't think where you get your horseflesh from,' called out Mr. Craig, as the cart drew up at the end of the stoop with a grind and a crash.

'Two leaders I brought down from Kafirland last trip I made. Wheelers—steady old chaps they are—have risen from the ranks. Jones picked 'em up for me in Durban when the last regiment left,' responded Dare, as he swung himself out of the cart to help his wife down.

'I wish they were a little steadier yet. My hair is all tumbling down, and no one would think this dress was white when I started,' she remarked ruefully, as she jumped into his extended arms.

Mr. Craig came hurrying along to the end of the veranda to receive her.

'Beautiful old soul! A picture of a man, truly!' thought Mrs. Dare, as she glanced admiringly up at him.

Mr. Craig had his Sunday manners and his weekday manners, that he would whip in and out of his pocket much as a chameleon changes his hues; but it was with his most stately bow that he took her hand now, and in his quietest, deepest voice that he greeted her; then, bending his silvered head, added a few low kind words.

Her lips quivered slightly, and she let the sunlight of her eyes rest upon him for a moment with a truly grateful look.

'Rock,' said Mrs. Dare, coming out on the veranda half an hour later, and finding Dare with his heels in the air, his chair tilted back against the wall, and a pipe in his mouth, alone—'Rock, did you hear what Mr. Craig said to me when we came?'

'That he was unutterably delighted to see you?'

'I don't mean that, tiresome,' responded

Mrs. Dare, seating herself on the arm of his chair. 'How he spoke so nicely of poor dear Cator, and said that he was so sorry I had had to lose her.'

'Yes.'

'Well, Rock, I have been having a long talk with him since on the back veranda, and you have no idea, until you come to talk to him seriously, what nice ideas and opinions he has about many things, and what a fund of common-sense. He has read and thought deeply, too. I dare say strangers think, as I did at first, that he is simply a jolly sort of soul, a woman-hater, and amusing when he rides his hobby (which everyone, by-the-way, is not); but they are vastly mistaken.'

'No; he is a many-sided man, and a clever one. But I don't know that you are a competent judge, madam, although you look so " wondrous wise;" for you bring the best side of everyone uppermost, as a rule. Some people do, Cara.'

'Rock, when you flatter, I am aghast! You used to be a very decent courtier, but nowadays you have grown so rough and shaggy, that when you fall back on these ancient gambols I tremble like poor Mrs. Craig with her cocks, and think " something will happen." Even if your allegation were true, it does not defeat my argument. You cannot bring out of people what they have not got in them.'

'True, O queen!'

'When I have heard him bullying and routing round *à la* colony,' continued Mrs. Dare thoughtfully, ' I have wondered sometimes how his delicate, fragile little wife came to marry him, except for his appearance. She might have been afraid. But now I can quite see how he got over her.'

' This won't do ; I can't have him get over you,' said Dare, laying down his pipe with a smile.

' If you don't approve of these sort of tactics, why did you employ them yourself,

sir? Yes, Rock—now, don't say you didn't
—in a different kind of way, and, ah me ! if
I were dead to-morrow, would go and
employ them again.'

Rockingham Dare smiled, but his eyes
rested on his lovely wife with that deep
fidelity shining in their depths which was
the dominant trait in his character.

'Ah dear!' sighed Mrs. Dare, 'if men
only knew and remembered the effect on
women of being "nice," they would slay
like David, instead of like Saul.'

'It is a merciful provision of Nature, then,
we should not be able to get about for the
heaps of slain. It is bad enough as it
is!'

'You conceited, abominable lump! As
if we took any of you, except out of pity—
ever! A man is a thing one looks down
on, on principle. That one would scarcely
notice, in fact, if he did not shove himself
in our way.'

'I guess it was a pity you didn't stick to

that, darling, when he didn't shove,' said Dare insinuatingly.

'Why, we did, of course.'

'Eh? How about the Garden of Eden?'

Mrs. Dare, with her head in the air, went along the stoop.

'Rock, I feel so disgusted with you, I could not speak another word to you—if it was to save my life! Oh! Mr. Seymour, is it you?' As that gentleman came strolling round the corner with a huge bunch of roses in his hand. 'Not for me! How very kind of you—how can I thank you?'

'If they afford you a little pleasure I shall be more than thanked,' returned Seymour eagerly.

'How very beautiful! Glorious old Maréchal Niel, and those great dark crimson ones. Where did you get them?'

'I went to—town yesterday, and brought them out with me.'

'Rock, look at my roses! Is it not kind of Mr. Seymour? Are they not fine?'

'Yes, indeed. You will "dream you dwell in rosy bowers" now, Cara.'

'They will make my house lovely, Mr. Seymour; thank you so much. Ah, dear!' —with a sudden thought—'I shall not be there. What a pity!'

'Perhaps you could wear some of them,' said Seymour negligently. 'I think I have seen you wear flowers.'

'Perhaps I could,' answered Mrs. Dare, musing. 'Ah, I have a happy thought!' and the brown eyes sparkled happily up to his.

'Yes?' eagerly. 'Your thoughts are always happy.'

'We will *all* wear them! So lovely! It is a sin *one* should be wasted.'

CHAPTER II.

JACK PAYS A COMPLIMENT.

RS. DARE sat at the piano in the sitting-room, singing song after song. It was a fresh bright morning, with the air coming in softly and pleasantly at the open door, and lifting the yellow hair that lay in natural ripples upon her forehead.

A step came behind her, and Jack strolled up to the piano and stood leaning his elbow upon it.

Was he thinking that he had never seen a fairer picture than this lovely woman whose impassioned voice was filling the room, and likely to fill the senses of anyone who listened to it ? This woman with the masses of yellow hair, the fair skin, and the down-dropped eyelids with brown curling lashes, clothed in softly falling white, with the bunch of pomegranate-blossoms in her breast.

Then she looked up, with the deep earnest glance that would flash through her eyes when her heart was moved, and Jack wondered he had ever thought anything beautiful about her except her eyes.

He was used to her beauty—it was a picture that was almost part of his life, and they were old friends now ; but every now and then it struck him afresh and carried him back in memory to the day, now years ago, when as a youth he had first seen her. Somehow he had never forgotten that day —when he met her riding alone on the veldt, and she had stopped to ask him the way, and he had stood almost speechless, thinking that such a face and figure he had never seen or imagined out of his dreams. He had blundered sadly, he knew, and then

walked on with a feeling of dreamy pleasure,
and the glance of those wonderful dark eyes
seeming to draw his thoughts back like a
magnet.

. She had been in her early girlhood then
—now in the meridian of her beauty—and
Jack had long outlived those romantic
feelings ; but he looked at her sometimes
still, and became conscious of the subtle
bewildering pleasure which flows over us as
we gaze at the perfect sculpture or the rich-
hued painting, and we feel as if Satan indeed were behind us for once, and that our
feet were on the edge of those plains of
heaven that rest always bathed in the light
of perfect beauty, which is peace.

'Go on, please,' said Jack. 'Don't stop
because I have come.'

'I will not. I am not modest,' replied
Mrs. Dare, laughing.

'Suppose you asked me to paint you a
picture, you would see me overwhelmed by
it, for I should be conscious of my in-

capacity.   But I believe I *can* sing—and it is the joy of my life.'

'No mistake about that,' said Jack, dropping into a chair near the piano. ' I feel "hipped" this morning, and there are those buffaloes this afternoon—perhaps I'll never come back from them, you know.   So give me a real treat for once, Mrs. Dare ; sing your sweetest—something I have not heard before.'

'That is a nice, easy, modest request. Let me think.'   She struck a few plaintive chords, then she said : ' This song is in a book of Lady Constance Howard's, and I have found an accompaniment for it.   Tell me if you like it.'

It began thus :

> ' Won't you tell me, Dollie darling !
>   That you love none else but me ?
> For I love you, Dollie darling !
>   You are all the world to me.
> ' I must leave you, Dollie darling !
>   Tho' the parting gives me pain—
> When the stars shine, Dollie darling !
>   I will meet you here again.'

'Well,' said Mrs. Dare, after the third verse, looking demurely at the keys, 'do you like it? It is Mollie in the original, but I have improved upon the first letter, as you see.'

'Yes, I like it,' replied Jack, whose face had been shaded by his hand.

She looked up quickly at a certain ring of pain in his voice.

'Oh, Jack, what have I done!' she exclaimed, leaning across to him. 'I thought it would make you happy to hear that song.'

'It makes me happy to hear you sing anything,' said Jack gallantly, recovering himself with an effort.

'No; but is there anything wrong?'

She spoke in a soft whisper.

'Wrong?' muttered Jack, looking at her sympathetic face. 'Don't let us talk about it—it is all wrong.'

'I must talk about it just this once. You are so nice, and kind, and true, Jack; why doesn't she care for you?'

Jack jumped out of his chair and stood resting on the instrument, looking down at her. He hesitated, then said with a bitter laugh :

'Have you not heard love-tales enough in your life ? But I believe women are never tired of that sort of thing. A man is not so fond of talking of a cross-tie in his life.'

'Very well. Forgive me,' said Mrs. Dare, turning away with a rather hurt expression. 'Only I am such an old friend now, Jack, and——' with a soft sigh of reminiscence that stirred the scarlet flowers where they rested—'who should have sympathy with lovers, if not I ?'

'Don't be offended. I didn't mean it,' entreated Jack. 'I am always out of sorts now. Has not Rockingham told you anything ?'

'Not a word. I thought the course of true love was running smooth, outside a little parental frowning.'

'I will tell you,' said Jack, speaking

slowly, 'if you want to hear — why shouldn't I? If there is a woman in the world to whom I can tell things, it is you —I don't know why. Dollie is going to be married—to—well, to somebody else this day week——'

'Jack!' exclaimed Mrs. Dare, stepping back in astonishment. 'Oh, I am grieved! But '—very gently—' she loves you?'

'I ought rather to hope she doesn't, oughtn't I?' said Jack sadly.

'I don't know—that is hard to say.'

They stood in silence, for Mrs. Dare had risen now.

'Oh, I wish I could help you!' she said at last, wistfully. 'Jack, if I ever can, let me know; nothing will be too hard;' and she held out her hand to him. 'Besides, I have been happy, and for that reason I ought to help all others. And, please forgive that song; you know I would not have sung it for worlds, if I had known. You must have thought me so cruel.'

'Never mind, you could not tell,' said Jack, taking the soft hand in his, and looking down into the great eyes dewy with unshed tears, and at the sweet, sad mouth.

'One question,' continued Mrs. Dare—'I have often wanted to know. I heard she was very young—is she pretty?'

Was it those eyes that wrenched the answer from Jack's lips?

'She is pretty—*not beautiful as you are.*' Then, with a sudden rush of colour to his face, he dropped her hand. 'Oh, Mrs. Dare, I did not mean that!' And then Jack bit his lips. Was not the second blunder worse than the first?

She dropped her eyes. Perhaps she had known their power to urge men on to madness before to-day. She laughed gaily.

'Jack, I have always admired your intense truthfulness, but I am afraid it has been fostered at the expense of the complimentary arts. Never mind; in my vanity,

I will choose to believe that the first speech came from your heart, not the second !'

And with the radiant smile, which made her face, except in sad moments, such an ever-changing, winningly bright one, she left the room.

And Jack leant upon the piano, in a reverie.

'Well, I'm blowed !' remarked Freddy's voice from the little room that was used as a smoking-room, and opened off the sitting-room. 'If you are not big enough, and ugly enough, not to make such a fool of yourself !'

'Oh, you are there, are you ?' said Jack, with some dissatisfaction in his voice.

'Yes, I'm here. Now don't begin growling at me. I should like to know where I *am* to be ? Nowhere, it seems to me ! I go out on the stoop, shady side—I get enough of the sun in *my* life—there is Mr. Adair and that girl of his, handsome but wicious. She said something beastly to me,

of course. I forget what it was, but never
mind ; I have stored it up, and I intend to
pay her out for it some day. It struck me
Adair was yawning his head off—perhaps I
had to bear the brunt of that. He will
yawn and hook it too, I should think, when
he's married. I went into the arbour
then ; there was the mother and old More.
" Hush ! here's Freddy !" she said with a
jump, as I looked in. It didn't require
supernatural intelligence to discover they
were talking about me ; and as they relapsed
into dead silence, I could not quite hang on.
Then I looked up Seymour. As a rule he
is glad to see me, but I suppose he was
cross because he had to sit the sunny side ;
and he would not give me up one of the
three chairs he was using, though I told him
I could not stay there without, and he said
he was quite aware of that. Civil, wasn't
it ? But there is something gone wrong
with Seymour lately. I like him, you
know—I always did (though no one would

think so) ; but he is changing somehow.
He is losing his drawl, and he is not nearly
so amiable, nor so sleepy as he used to be.
You should have heard him swear last night
when Mrs. Dare was making up all those
button-holes for us, and she gave me the
leaves and stalks to throw away outside,
and, not seeing him in the dark, I threw
some over him.   As if they could hurt him !
And he never used to swear.   Do you remember his saying to you when you asked
him why he always said " Distasteful," it
was quiet and gentlemanlike ; did you think
he was going to exhaust himself saying
something with a big " D," as you were
always doing ?   Well,   then,'   continued
Freddy, in a deeply injured tone, ' I come
in here for a little peace and quietness,
where I can be in no one's way, possibly,
and you bite my head off—at least you
would if you had known I was there.'

' I don't care where you are,' said Jack
ungraciously.

'No, so long as I am not in your way. I never supposed you did. I say, Jack'—ir a more friendly voice—'if Mrs. Dare were to say half the pretty things to Seymour she does to you, I fancy he might not be so cross.'

'I cannot recall any "pretty things" Mrs. Dare ever said to me. I believe there is liking between us, always was. But then, you see, we are all friends, and Seymour is only an—outsider.'

'Hum, exactly. Oh, Jack!' said Freddy, taking a big stretch, and tapping his chest as his brother left the room ; 'and yet they say *I* am the sharp boy of this family !'

CHAPTER III.

NO VICTORIA CROSS FOR MODESTY.

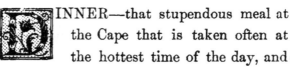INNER—that stupendous meal at the Cape that is taken often at the hottest time of the day, and which, if you have any personal antipathy to flies, or a weakly fancy for food that has not been buzzed over, is one long trial to your digestion and your temper—had once more been accomplished.

Mr. Craig had demonstrated clearly once again that 'Parliament' was quite wrong in its treatment of up-country matters—that it was too hard on the farmers and too light on the Kafirs. That the Home Government, to be sure, had a finger in the pie ; and what could the Home Government know about a question that puzzled clear-headed brains on the spot? He should like to ask the Home Government to stay a month at his place, to assist in the practical working of the estate, and hobnob with the Kafirs on their own mud-heaps, and then he might be inclined to listen with more respect to their ideas ; but, for his part, he believed by that time there would not be a rag of argument left between them. And they would see the Kafir as practical men saw him, not as fancy painted him to visionaries in Downing Street. And fewer missionaries would make their fortunes, and more traders and farmers would make theirs, which, considering that missionaries were certain of their recompense in the next world, and, according to them, no one else was, was a thing much to be desired.

Mr. More had a relation who was a missionary in the Fiji Islands, and the good that man had done was untold.

'My dear sir,' had thundered Mr. Craig,

bringing a heavy brown fist down on the table, '*have you ever been to the Fijis?* The whole affair lies in that nutshell. When you will bring me a man who has spent ten years of his life there, *and who is not a missionary*, to back your assertion, I will begin to turn it over in my mind. Before that, I care that for it!' And Mr. Craig cracked his fingers airily. 'It's all pooh-pooh and barney! I do not say there are not isolated instances — shining lights, I suppose you call 'em—but that don't leaven the batch. Look here, on the spot ; take the ordinary missionary and the ordinary Kafir, and they have a deteriorating effect on one another—to put it mildly. Mind, I've lived here—I haven't sat at home in London and painted romances—I've lived 'em! And I say it, and there are few impartial men who have travelled who won't back me—that instead of the missionary dragging the Kafir up to heaven with him, the Kafir is much more likely to drag the

missionary down *there !'* And emphasizing
this argument, Mr. Craig put his foot heavily
on his pointer's nose lying by his chair,
which created a momentary diversion before
the battle raged afresh.

Miss Wynyard, having gazed at her host's
vivacity with wide-open curious eyes and
turned her back on Robin, who had apparently fallen under her displeasure, entered
into conversation with Rockingham Dare
on the subject of horses, in which she con-
descended to be interested.

À propos of this, she launched into a
narrative of what she was going to do in
England shortly ; of the extensive accom-
modation of the stables at Holm Lea, of
which Mr. Adair had told her ; of her intentions respecting those stables ; of the hunters
and the thoroughbreds she was about to fill
them with, and of her optimist views of life
and arrangements generally.

This speech, travelling to the end of the
table, was received by Freddy with an

appreciative grin, and a whisper to Mrs. Dare :

' That is what ails her ladyship ; she thinks she is going to England, and going to take possession of poor Adair's place, and be such a howling swell, she cannot get over it.'

· ' I think I would rather be to the " manner born," and then it might not occupy my mind so much,' responded Mrs. Dare, with a twist of her white throat.

' Great heavens !' was Robin's inward comment with a thrill of dismay, and he looked anxiously at Dare ; but that gentleman was listening with courteous interest to the lady's confidences, and nothing could be gleaned from his expressionless face as to whether he approved or was staggered thereat. 'I have fancied existence on many different lines,' mused Robin, as he shivered under the ornate account of his old place that went on glibly flowing from his *fiancée's* lips ; 'but it certainly did not

occur to me that it might be spent studying
people's faces to see how my wife's utter-
ances strike them.' Aloud, he said gently :
'You must recollect that Mr. Dare is only
lately "out," and so has hardly had time
to forget what the country places of old
England are like. In fact, I suspect he re-
members much better than I do ; he has
lived there long since I have, I fancy.'

Robin's tones, if gentle, were decided ;
and if a look could have annihilated him,
Miss Wynyard bestowed that look upon
him. But Dare quietly took the cue, and
gradually and determinedly led the conversation into a more general channel.

Miss Wynyard's experience of the world
had been decidedly limited, but she possessed a fine inherent knowledge of such
things to steer by. The lack of a mother,
a childhood spent in India, and a girlhood
in a small South African town, might have
been difficulties in some people's path. She
resolved they should be none in hers ; in

fact, she planned and schemed for the
present and the future in a manner that
might have astonished Robin very much, if
he could only have seen into the workings·
of her mind.

Englishmen of good family were by no
means as plentiful as oranges in South
Africa, but they were scattered one here
and there, and there were always some
birds of passage. Miss Wynyard had fine
powers of observation, and she knew the
creed of a man of Robin's stamp as well as
if she had been brought up in it, or to
sympathize with it. The man who has any
adaptability, and adaptability is the secret
of success, will put aside for the time old-
world prejudices and ideas on his entrance
into the new world, and only on meeting a
kindred spirit will he intentionally lift the
veil ; but such surface-acting could not
impose on a girl possessing Miss Wynyard's
keen discrimination. While she was casting
the net over Robin she deemed it politic to·

defer to his opinion, and carried it to the extent of falling in with certain ideas which Robin fondly believed to be so carefully concealed that nothing short of a natural sympathy could have discovered their existence. But that time had gone by. The calm courtesy and attention with which he treated her were so apart from any succumbing to her fascinations, that it only irritated her into attempts to find a joint in his armour. She rated her own charms very highly, not without reason ; and so she was led at times into believing that his words, 'I have no love to give,' had not been a mere figure of speech holding a wider meaning, but a simple statement of a fact.

On this particular day Robin was engaged in studying her also in a way that she would have been most unwilling to give him credit for. He was a travelled man of the world, with wide and liberal ideas, he was prone to consider. When the subject was his own wife, he found that those ideas were more exclusive than he had commonly supposed them to be. He found himself narrowly watching her—speaking and moving with decision, with that knowledge of good and evil, of the seamy side and the bright side stamped upon her that somehow does not harmonize with the ideal of opening girl-hood—and his taste, which was old-world and strict, disapproved. She had none of the languor of the Anglo-Indian; she was very handsome, and stately enough, with a taking vitality about her beauty; but Robin had met her hitherto chiefly at entertainments in a mixed society, and now, seen in the quiet of home-life—that searching test —he compared her as he was apt to do all women with one, and found her wanting.

' Poor Holm Lea,' thought Robin, with a loving thought to the old place and the old name, and a wistful pang of memory that flew to the graceful gentlewoman who he once hoped would reign there, and bear his name—in whose every movement, in whose soft voice, the good old blood betrayed itself—who bore the Hall-mark, that intangible something in body and mind, that indicates breeding, even to the careless observer. The Wynyards during two generations had figured, he knew, in the Indian army; held—he had learnt since his engagement—as second-rate men in that service, and whose origin, beyond it, was lost in obscurity. Robin felt, as he looked at the girl beside him, that it would be unwise to probe that obscurity.

'Bah! we cannot have everything in this world; am I getting insular in my old age?' he thought to himself with a fine scorn, which no doubt was a comforting thing in its way. 'Why should I object to her talking about Holm Lea ?—it is her part of the bargain. If she were to talk about me now, I might reasonably complain!'

And at this pleasant stage of his reflections he was not sorry when they all rose from the table, and the massive form of Michel Steen filled up the doorway.

He had come with his dogs and his ' boys,' his cousins and his friends, to join the buffalo-hunt. So he wore an air of great importance, of furious business on his jolly face, that gave it a lugubrious appearance ; and he was fussy—very—and in a hurry, and they must get off—get off, and so he would not come in, and sat on the ' stoop ' instead, drinking Boer brandy, with lines of thought and frowns of anxiety on his brow.

His Scotch cart was there, with half a dozen buffalo dogs lying by it, and laden with the guns and the food and the various necessaries for the expedition. Presently the Craigs' Scotch cart came round, drawn by four sleek oxen, and was similarly laden; and then the horses, showing subdued excitement. There was much swearing at the ' boys,' and everybody yelling and nobody listening; and there was as much fuss and as much dust and as much delibera-

tion as if it had been Lord Wolseley starting
for the Soudan—and a gradual progression
to a triumphal start! To be sure, whether
you are going to the Soudan or to a buffalo-
hunt, you must take everything you want
with you, as the chances are against your
coming back for it; and the buffaloes, at
least, will be willing to wait and ripen—
while you put your house in order.

Some such idea Jack endeavoured to
convey to Michel Steen when he found him
waxing impatient with wonder as to why
the Englishmen, who had so many more
hours to prepare in, must delay the party
already on the road. But at last the men
in their rough shooting-jackets and gaiters
crowded into the dining-room from their
bedrooms, and the ladies, catching the excitement, hovered round to see them off.

'Mrs. Dare, you gave everyone a "button-
hole" last night, except your humble servant. Will you repair your negligence
to-day by giving me a badge I may carry to

victory?' remarked Seymour, as he stood by
her.

'Indeed! I beg your pardon. Not one
of your own roses? That *was* an over-
sight. But, you know, you are not the first
brave, worthy man who has failed to get
his honours through the fact that there
is no Victoria Cross for modesty, whatever
there may be for pluck.'

'Ah! Then one must push into the
front rank when you are distributing decora-
tions. You never look beyond——'

'Cela va sans dire! Let who can be
brave. *Push* — you know the rest, or
will learn it in the world some day.'

And Mrs. Dare took a rose from the vase
on the table.

'There it is! May it be fortunate!
Remember, these are practical days; the
knight of old used to bring back honour
and glory—they are barren. Bring *me* a
buffalo!'

A shower of leaves decorated the floor.

'Alas for my buffalo! Throw it away, Mr. Seymour; it is unlucky.'

'No,' said Seymour, with a smile. 'Like honour, it may be barren, but I'd rather hold to it than to a more profitable flower.'

'You are behind the age you live in——'

'Not beyond your sympathies, therefore, I trust?'

'Ah no! my sympathies travel in that direction. Rock dear, do promise me you will be careful with that rifle, and '—in a whisper—' stand *behind* everyone. They do shoot so wildly.'

'Is there much danger?' asked Miss Wynyard of Mrs. Dare, as they stood together on the stoop.

'I believe not; but I am always nervous.'

'Danger?' echoed Freddy, who had overheard it. '*Miles* of it! Why, last time—no, that before (like consumption, it takes every other one)—a fellow got in the line of

24—2

fire, and was shot in the leg just as the buffaloes were coming on. And, of course, when they did come,' added Freddy gravely, ' it was a case of squash-pie. He melted away like jelly in the sun.'

' Shut up your rubbish !' growled Jack.

Miss Wynyard stood by her lover, and her face was not quite so statuesque as usual.

' You will run no risks?' she said, looking up at him.

He was by far the handsomest man there, and might well have evoked a woman's pride, if not her love, as he stood by her side with the proud, careless grace that was always in his bearing, and the pleasant smile on his lips which, in its very mournfulness, seemed to add attraction to a face that was really noble.

He turned his deep grey eyes on her, that always contradicted his gay, light tones.

' Do not be anxious—there is no danger for any of us ; and as for me, for ten years and more I have borne a charmed life. Is it likely I shall not be able to guard it—with a reason for doing so?'

'Ah! that is the dangerous moment, when you must be very careful it does not slip from your grasp,' said Mrs. Dare, shaking her head. 'It is the man whose life is done and over that never finds it easy to lose it, Mr. Adair.'

'I never contradict any sentiment that falls from a fair lady's lips,' replied Robin, with a meaning smile, that lingered on his face when he had shaken hands with his betrothed and mounted his horse.

She watched him, with the faint colour tinging her cheeks and her great eyes softened.

'That image is waking up,' remarked Freddy to Dare, as they drew back from the stoop to allow the others to mount.

'What did he say, exactly?' asked Robin.

'*My* foot in it, of course. You would think I had got ten feet. Anybody else

would have seen him at their elbow,'
groaned Freddy.

'He said,' returned Dare, as they rode
on after waving their adieus, 'that he sus-
pected it would be a case of " Pygmalion
and Galatea " over again. Excuse it, the
sentiment is not mine.'·

'Bless him!' muttered Freddy. 'I love
that man as a brother.'

Robin laughed. Then he said, bitterly :

'You think interest was shown in me?
Not likely. A man like me, you see, can
be picked up every day. Holm Lea now,
as you heard of it, must strike you as something unusual—worth looking after.'

Dare looked with a queer smile under
his straight brows at his companion.

'I dare say it is a fine old place,' he said
quietly.

'I am fond of it—naturally,' returned
Robin, with a sigh; 'but, like all things
near one's heart, do not care to hear its
name taken in vain.'

Jack and Seymour, and old Michel Steen, had taken the rearguard, and were whipping up the stragglers. They were the last to leave, and Mr. Craig stood on the stoop with his eyes twinkling, and roared out :

' Michel! Hou! Hou! Wacht een beeche! You have forgotten something after all.' And Mr. Craig waved aloft the empty brandy-bottle on the stoop.

This was an old joke, and the jolly Dutchman did not withhold the guffaw that was its due, nor the remark :

' I gib it, I gib it you!'

Seymour took off his hat with a sweeping bow to Miss Wynyard and Mrs. Dare, where they still stood together.

' It suggests the "Dream of Fair Women," he remarked to Jack.

' Oh, bother the women!' said Jack. ' Let's think of the buffaloes!'

CHAPTER IV.

ROUND THE CAMP FIRE.

 VERY different scene. High level lands on the top of a range of mountains lying under a brilliant moonlight, to which the sportsmen had attained after many hours of weary, winding, climbing travel. Grass veldt, broken up here and there by deep kranzes, lay all round their camp, and isolated trees and thickets of bush were features of the landscape. Wild, and grand, and still it lay under the moon's rays, and the camp-fires blazed merrily, and spirits were high with anticipation. 'Spoor' was thick, and supper was cooking, and what more did fatigued sportsmen require? The horses were being turned adrift, knee-haltered, and the oxen, under care of a Kafir, who had watered them, were driven off to a place rich in pasture, from which it was hoped that even their ingenuity might fail to extricate themselves.

There were many fleys formed by the late rains, and two adventurous spirits, Jack and young Ruben Steen, had betaken themselves to a distant one, overshadowed by a big tree, where, with their rifles lying along the branches, they rested, hoping thus to have a first shy at the buffaloes.

'It is only a ghost of a chance,' Jack had remarked, 'for the brutes drink at sundown ; but fellows *have* trapped them so, why not we ?'

'Look sharp, do—don't talk about it !' returned Freddy. 'The pot is nearly boiling, and if you don't look alive the meat won't be here in time.'

'Will you come, Dare ?' Jack had asked, as they moved off.

'Thanks. No. I don't mind sitting out for bucks, but I'm hanged if I am going to sit out for buffaloes. Bring one back, and I will eat my words with all the pleasure in life.'

'Don't go to sleep and tumble down into the fley!' yelled Seymour after them; and with this parting benediction they had started.

The others sat round the fire, which roared and roared, and so required a Kafir to be constantly on his knees feeding it; and they boiled their coffee and drank it, and ate the beef they had brought up with them, and threw the crumbs about, which the dogs picked up. The dogs were satisfied, as they expected little else on these expeditions. They knew by experience that their 'grub' is usually left at home, that they get a feed before they start, and must depend on their own sharpness and buffalo-luck for the next. Then they filled their pipes, and the Kafirs changed places with the dogs, and gathered up the fragments and boiled *their* coffee, and grinned and gurgled at a respectful distance from their masters.

When the pipes were lighted, and the fire had comfortably warmed the limbs that the chill damps of the African night had cramped, they began to dive into the recesses of memory for stories wild and unfettered as the scenery.

Robin told of an adventure with a polar bear in the regions of eternal snow, when he had been two days without food, while the bear, apparently, had been the same, and it was a race between them which should relieve the other's hunger.

Which Dare improved upon in a thrilling tale of a black Bruin with cubs that he stumbled upon asleep in North America, who chased him until, in his dismay, and from looking behind him instead of in front, he fell down a precipice, to the great disgust of the bear, and hung in a bush

half-way down with a broken arm, and
suffered untold things; until, aided by
unexampled luck, and the winding path of
a rivulet, he climbed to the top again, and
with a courage that should have given him
the Legion of Honour—if that was not the
perquisite of sitting at home—followed the
bear's trail, made it finally square with her,
shooting her with his left hand, and warmed
a cub in his bosom to rejoice his comrades;
and later secured her skin and landed it in
Europe with this Baron Munchausen tied
on to it, to thrill fair ladies whose slippered
feet would tread its folds, little dreaming
how, through starvation and gore and sweats
of agony, this prize had been won!

The Dutchmen clicked and wondered,
and the general company admired and inquired and cavilled, as such companies will
do.

And then old Michel, with deliberate
accents and many a striking gesture, thrilled
them afresh in his own language with a

story of a midnight 'trek' through the lion
country, on a trip to the Diamond Fields in
the good old times, when transport-riding
lined pockets much more than did diamonds,
and when the Transvaal was not to the
front, and a lion stood and looked at a man
because he did not know what he was—by
God! When this lion had sufficiently
curdled his hearers' blood, he tranquilly
submitted to a waggon-whip—a thing, also,
he had not seen before—and faded from
view ; and then everyone took breath and
smoothed down perpendicular hairs, and lay
and pondered on these travellers' yarns.
Then Jack and Ruben came in disappointed
and hungry, and the fire was stirred up
afresh ; and while they ate they told how
they had seen a buck crossing the open with
something after him, that they believed to
be a tiger—but the moon, of course, went
under a cloud at the instant. And how
they could have shot them easily—Jack
having arranged to take the buck, and

Ruben the tiger—if their guns had been in their hands instead of on the branches; and what a lesson it was to a fellow, by Jove ! never to put his gun down for an instant, and always to keep it at full-cock.

'Talking of "full-cock,"' remarked Robin, who had lighted another pipe and rolled himself into the warmest corner, 'was it on this veldt anywhere that a man was killed on a buffalo trip—shot by his brother, I believe—owing to that same "full-cock" predilection ? It was in the papers—did you ever hear the story ?'

' Ja, ja !' and ' Neen, neen, not hier !' came from the Dutchmen.

'No, not this part,' replied Jack. 'It was down Port Elizabeth way.'

' Ah, so it was,' said Robin.   ' He died there, didn't he ?'

' Yes, he died in hospital—of hemorrhage, I fancy ; but I don't feel very clear about that part of the story. The rest of it I remember well.   I was round the coast at the time, and I heard it from a fellow, who heard it from another fellow, who got it from one who either saw it or had it straight-hand from one of the party.'

'Never heard of a thing getting about like that before,' murmured Freddy, from where he rested his back luxuriously against a sneezewood log.

Jack shook his fist at him and went on :

'It must have lain heavy on the man that did it.'

'Tell us ; it will pass away the time, and then we shall be ready to turn in,' requested ·his hearers.

'Fire away,' said Freddy.

'All right,' and folding his arms and gazing into the fire, Jack began his narrative :

'It was a party of fellows—just as we might be, you know—only I think they were all Dutch. Anyway they were used to the veldt, and often went after buffalo. The man who was shot was in the prime

of life, and a keen sportsman. The man
who did it, a younger brother on a visit to
him. It was said that he was known to be
careless with firearms. They had camped
the night before, and started after the
buffaloes at daylight. But they were not
lucky, so they divided into two parties, and
went their separate ways—the man who was
shot, his brother, and a boy keeping
together. It was afternoon before they
sighted any buffaloes. They were going
along in single file between two walls of
high bush, when suddenly, round a turn,
they saw before them the open veldt and
the herd grazing. They were still within
the bush, so the first man stopped sharply,
and made them a sign to crouch; at the
instant he did so, the next man's gun went
off, and the charge entered his leg, well
above the knee. How it happened will
never be accurately known. The brother
always maintained he was carrying his gun
at half-cock, but that a twig caught it and

turned the trigger—this, we know, is well-nigh an impossibility. What was supposed generally was that the gun was at full-cock, and from the start the man gave on seeing the buffaloes he either unconsciously pressed the trigger, or the jerk did it. The wound was a frightful one, the whole charge of heavy shot tearing the limb in a ghastly way. What was to be done? They were many miles from camp, and the other party had gone they knew not where. Finally they sent the boy back to camp with instructions to bring on the other party, if they had arrived, to carry the wounded man back; or, if not, to return with the two Kafirs left there with blankets and restoratives—for it was mid-winter, and very cold. The boy started, and half an hour after he had left it came on a soaking rain. In the middle of the night that stopped and turned to a frost—and so the night wore away. Hour after hour the brother watched, and waited, and shouted in vain—no help came.

The boy, unused to the veldt, and bewildered by the rain and darkness, lost his way, and did not reach the camp until after daylight. So under the rain and frost, without a drop of brandy or a rag to cover him, he passed the night. It was midday before the party discovered the two men ; from day-light they had been wandering about in search of them. They got him to camp with endless toil, and then it was again nightfall. They had no means of getting him down to the valley ; the road was vile, of course—fifteen miles of it—and they had only a small Scotch cart. But they knew that somewhere there was a short-cut that ran on the other side of the mountains, leading down to the opposite end of the valley.

'The Kafirs thought they could find this track, which would bring them assistance quickly, and they started at once. It was a clear night — another frost — but they managed to miss it. However, when morning dawned, they struck the right direction, and made for the valley. But they never hit upon the track, so at midday they found themselves above the village, truly, but on the top of high cliffs, with a sheer descent to the river-bed, and no means of getting down. Here they capered, and shouted, and waved their blankets, but for a long time no one saw them; besides, it was white Kafir time, and they were supposed to be going through some of their antics. Hours passed before they were successful. At last, it seemed to have occurred to a man, whose son had joined the buffalo party, that there might be something wrong, and he sent up a fellow who knew the path to bring them down. No time was lost then, and men went up with what was necessary; but again there was a difficulty in finding the camp, and they only reached it at daylight. To bring the man down by the short-cut was at once decided upon, but his sufferings by this time were great, and the stretcher made slow progress. The day was well advanced when they reached the top of the cliffs —triumphant! One glance below showed the river boiling at the foot of the crags! To cross was impossible; so they spent another night of misery and suspense, and in the morning found it was only a flush, and the thing might be done. They got him down, how, I suppose, they hardly knew, and started him in a waggon for his own home, eight miles away. What the poor wretch went through in that waggon on such roads, with his wound in the condition it was, it is appalling even to think. They should have taken him at once to hospital, but instead, they took him to his farm, where he passed the night, the women wailing and weeping over him, Dutch fashion. Next day some of the more go-ahead inhabitants took it up, and urged his going at once to try for his life. "No; he had suffered enough—he would stay there and die." For his wife and children's sake they persuaded him over, and some English fellows drove him, lending a conveyance and padding it up, and so got him to the station. Tenderly enough they did it, I was told; but it was ten miles, and he fainted several times on the journey. Thence they sent him down by rail, and when he got to the hospital, as might have been expected, his wound was rotten and mortified. He underwent amputation, and died shortly.— Now,' added Jack, 'if my tale is not sufficiently ghastly, let me remark that the boy who was with them at the time was his own son, and that he had lately married again.'

' That will do,' remarked Freddy; ' quite enough, thank you. I shan't sleep a wink to-night if you give us any more grislies.'

' He must have shaken hands with Death gladly,' said Robin gravely.

' Poor fellow ! What a case of a life being '' called in '' !' remarked Dare.

'Just so ; the doctor's opinion was that with his wonderful strength they might have saved his life easily at first. But, bless you, what's the use of life to a man in this country with one leg ?'

CHAPTER V.

BUFFALOES TO THE FORE.

T break of day the camp was astir.

The Englishmen were not so sharp about shaking off their slumbers, so the Dutchmen vigorously routed them out ; as they shook themselves together when the chill grey dawn was breaking, Seymour was of opinion that there were pleasanter things than buffalo-hunting, here below.

'It is not all jam now,' he said ruefully, studying the scene outside through a hole in his blanket ; 'but I suppose it will be jolly enough to talk about when it is over.'

Freddy was unusually silent ; he was on

the look-out for snakes, and felt a little
depressed by an incident of the night
before.   He had been nodding away on his
sneezewood stump, and capsized it back-
wards ; there was a rush and a cry from
the Kafirs as his heels were seen in the air,
and hugging the ground under the stump
lay a small grey snake with red marks all
down the back.   There was a fine commo-
tion until it was killed and quartered.

' It must have been within a couple of
inches of your leg all the evening !' cried
Dare.

' A darned bad snake !' said Jack shakily ;
for he was very fond of his merry brother.

The Dutchmen, with lugubrious but kindly
faces, assured him that if that snake had
bitten him it would have been all up with
him, away from Croft's tincture and such
like charms.

' There is always the knife,' groaned
Seymour, sunk in gloom from the absence
of cushions, and brandies and soda.

' The Kafirs know what to do,' remarked Robin.

' Ay, they do, the brutes ! but it is their secret—they'd let you die sooner than trot it out ! In this case, however, I should have set to work throttling them, and hoped to squeeze it through at last,' returned Jack fiercely.

' It is a plant on the veldt they use chiefly,' said Dare. ' I forget the name, but there is a description of it published—I should know it.'

' Whatever they know is sure and sartin,' said Jack. ' Catch a nigger dying of snake-bite !'

But in Freddy's dreams puff-adders and cobras and red reptiles and black chased one another and him, and in the morning his nerves had not quite recovered their tone ; and as he rolled wearily out of the big blanket in which he had passed the night, his shrewd bright face looked pinched and haggard.

But the mountain air was invigorating, so that spirits waxed cheerier as soon as they had swallowed some hastily prepared coffee and biscuits. Seymour even scouted Jack's kindly suggestion ' that he would like to go home to his mother.'

' Now, Seymour, this is your maiden hunt, so you must take home a trophy. Don't let it be one of us, though! The way you carry that complex big bore of yours is apt to make one shudder,' suggested Dare.

' It is so ex-cee-ding-ly heavy,' replied Seymour.

' Ah, these wonderful new machines, clumbered up with costly trappings, and warranted to slay the man in the moon, are always—rot !' replied Dare, passing his hand affectionately along the smooth dark barrel of his own plain and workmanlike weapon.

' Who is your maker?' asked Seymour.

' Remington. But this rifle is quite an

old servant now. I saw an " Express " at
the house yesterday—whose was it?'

'Mine,' answered Robin. 'I brought
half a dozen shooting-irons of one kind and
another, and I have seen nothing; not even
the tips of a buck's ears.'

' No; they don't keep 'em on the verandas
here,' said Seymour. 'I have found that
very disappointing myself.'

Michel Steen here announced that he was
ready, and they moved off under his orders.
Like grey ghosts they glided over the veldt,
the dogs keeping to heel, and Michel pick-
ing up some 'spoor' and rejecting other,
muttering here and there, then throwing up
his head with a keen look round the country
and going ahead almost at a trot.

About a mile had been covered, when he
stopped short with a low exclamation, pointing to the ground :

' P-s-t-t ! Hik !' The others crowded
round. 'See—but now. It crumbles still
—there!' he said in Dutch.

With various expressions of delight they looked at the ' spoor,' on one side of which the soil was still shaking, and everyone's breath came a little faster.

Moving on slower, with greater care than before, Michel at last reached the edge of a miry pool where the rain had collected in a hollow, and the edges were trodden into slime. As he looked up with an expression of triumph, there was a rush in the bush, and a buck bounded out, almost into Seymour's arms.

'Good heavens!' he exclaimed, dropping his rifle.

But as the animal turned within a couple of yards he stooped for the weapon, and the report sounded over the plain.

The buck ran a few yards with a rush, then he stopped and staggered, and like a flash Freddy's little dog was on him, pinning him by the nose. The buck made a furious dig downward with his horns, then, rearing up his head, sharply shook the dog,

till it seemed as if he must clear himself.
It was but for a second, then, with a cry
and a stagger, he fell down on his knees
and toppled over on his side, just as Michel
Steen gave the word to his own dogs.

Seymour stood staring, feeling all the
sportsman's exultation as the wild game in
a wild land falls for the first time before his
rifle.

'What the devil you do that for?' exclaimed old Michel. 'We shall see no herd
now.'

'I forgot the buffaloes,' said Seymour
apologetically, coming down from the
heights. 'I'm sure I'm sorry, but — in
fact, I don't think I thought of anything.'

'Well, it was a temptation,' said Dare
kindly; 'and you are lucky, with a bush-
buck ram to your own cheek, first go off.'

'Clever little chap! Good little chap!'
cried Freddy affectionately to his terrier,
who was frisking about wild with excitement. 'Did he wonder why we didn't

shoot ?   Asses you thought us, didn't you, Snap ?'

'Wel, hij moet lig bij daare' (Well, he must lie there), said Michel thoughtfully, when the buck lay dead, and they had looked him over.

'And now, Seymour, give your gun a holiday,' suggested Jack ; 'for we should like a buffalo. We did not come this distance to look for buck.'

Grumbling and growling still, Michel Steen cruised round for a while, then he held up his hand suddenly, and they all listened.

From afar off came a dull sound. It might be a snort, it might be a stamp—it was impossible to say—but it betrayed the neighbourhood of some living thing. Then Michel listened still, with the keen ears that were trained to interpret such sounds.

'Right !' he said at last in Dutch. 'Right ! It is open country over there—no cover— we must do the best here.'

The dogs, with pricked ears and quivering noses, were listening and sniffing at the air. Michel's were valuable dogs, perfectly trained ; two had the appearance of half-bred bloodhounds, with magnificent black jowls ; the others, keener-nosed, deep tawny, and agile, were of the regular Boer breed.

Over the fley hung an old big thorn, and a space farther to the right another grew out of a thicket of bush.

Michel, Ruben, and Freddy swung themselves up into the thorn.

' I have no love for trees,' remarked Dare, taking his place in the bush, and the others followed him.

Michel growled a few words to his dogs, and they were off, swift and silent ; and with their rifles resting across their arms the hunters waited.

The sun was just gilding the veldt with his first pale rays, the wind came rushing wild and fresh across their faces, the rich sense of *living* which excitement brings—that men dare peril gladly to attain to it—

was full upon them. And they knew that
an hour of life on a mountain-top at day-
break in South Africa, with the glorious
climate of early spring, with the far-stretching blue sky meeting the green-swelling
veldt on the bold horizon, with a trusty
rifle in your hold, and a herd of coveted
game at no immeasurable distance, is a
thing to be desired and remembered. An
hour whose subtle charm will flash back to
them in far different scenes, as capricious
memory touches an unbidden chord ; for
to such hours of deep life—from which
trivialities are cast out—do men's hearts
turn in longing covetous remembrance to
reap a thrill of second-hand delight, after
years have rolled by, and existence, maybe,
is no more unfettered or glorious.

Awhile, and then there was a sudden, a
yelling bay of hounds, a thunder of flying
hoofs, and the silence of the land was
broken by a thousand echoes ; the herd
was rushing headlong towards the hunters.

Another instant, and they could see them away beyond with tossing manes, their horns tearing the ground which they scattered round them, their tails in the air —while they snorted and stamped and wheeled round the dogs, sweeping down with the thunder of a host, or halting as if in dismayed wrath at the daring of their pursuers.

But, presently, the dogs separated some two or three, and gradually distancing them from the others, drove them furiously along until the main body of the herd wheeled and went capering off. Then the dogs brought up the others, slowly but surely, by many a cunning dodge to the tree where their master was seated. Within two hundred yards of it they lost one, and two dogs went after him to turn him ; but he had got well ahead, and they were seen no more. The remainder of the dogs came on driving a buffalo, who had a big calf at her side, until near the tree, when they sharply deployed to stop her, and then Michel Steen took a steady aim behind the shoulder and fired ; Jack's gun also rang out from the bush at his side. The buffalo fell on her knees shot through the heart, which brought them all with a cheer to the spot. The calf hesitated, and Freddy knelt down and took careful aim at him.

'Why did you do that? Why not let him off—poor devil?' asked Jack, as the shot struck the ground, and he galloped off in terror.

'I did not want to kill him,' said Freddy disappointedly. 'It occurred to me to have him and tame him.'

'Bless my soul! Are you going to keep a menagerie? You have a blue-buck tame now, and two monkeys, and the baboon.'

'That's it. I am going to start a rival Barnum, and give the "gov" notice. I'm convinced his tricks don't benefit my health. So I can pick up the "furniture" on the quiet and the cheap this way.'

' Perhaps we may be thankful if you don't die in your boots.'

Old Michel was radiant again ; it was a good morning's work before the sun was well up, although the buffalo was not a large one. The dogs sat round with lolling tongues and frothing jaws, and dogs and people began to think about breakfast. The camp was at no great distance, so they agreed to return there, and set to work skinning the buffalo before the carcase should get stiff ; and finally landed in camp two hours later with a little meat and great appetites. The Kafirs were then directed to where the two carcases lay, and sent to bring in the buck and the buffalo-joints and hide.

When breakfast was over, and they had rested and smoked, and the Kafirs had come in, they proposed to start afresh. They were evidently in luck's way, and Robin and Dare were both anxious to have their turn.

26—2

Michel Steen and his son decided to remain in the camp. The other Dutchmen took the dogs and went off in one direction, while the Englishmen, having made up their minds to stalk the buffaloes, mounted their horses and rode towards the point where they were last seen. They took the two Kafirs with them, and struck the track by a cross-path, and rode on some miles. They reached some bush, and, as there were signs that the herd had settled to grazing again, they dismounted, and Seymour, who did not care to go on, remained with one Kafir in charge of the horses, and the other followed the advancing party. With their rifles over their shoulders, they tramped steadily on, listening and hoping for some sound of the chase. But all was dead stillness, and the sun was high, and the buffaloes seemed to have vanished from the face of the earth.

They stopped at last, and held a consultation. The last half-mile they had been going as silently as they might on a winding buck-path through thick bush, and they now gladly stood upright as a change from the strain of constant stooping.

' The bush is much more open,' remarked Dare ; ' we must be near the edge of it, and there must be a bit of open country beyond. Perhaps we shall sight them there.'

' It is not long since they passed over the open—before we got into this tangle,' said Robin.

' There is a tree over there !' cried Freddy. ' Let us climb it, and get a long view !'

' I shall go on on this path,' said Dare. ' I shall see as quickly as you, for it will take you some time to reach that tree.'

' You won't see so far,' cried Freddy triumphantly; and so they parted.

The tree, a huge yellow-wood, stood at the edge of the bush away to their left, and Robin was the first to reach it. He swarmed up a stout branch, followed by the others.

'It is open!' he cried. 'Ah, there is Dare, but no ghost of a buffalo!'

They all looked out eagerly — Robin wedged in a fork of the branch, with his rifle over his arm; Jack and Freddy, having left their guns at the foot of the tree, went on climbing higher.

The sun was glinting on the emerald veldt; a little to their right, Dare was walking leisurely across the open with a free swinging step and his rifle across his shoulder; clumps of bush straggled here and there, but it was a bit of beautiful veldt, covered by short, bright spring grass. There was a stretch of open, a piece of rising ground in front, then a hollow, then another rise.

'Jehosophat!' exclaimed Jack, whose eyes had been wandering over the country from his higher perch. 'Look! See! The buffaloes! In that hollow—lying down.

Why, Dare is walking into the middle of them. Somebody shout and stop him!' he added excitedly.

' Are you sure?' asked Robin.

' Certain.'

Jack put his hands to his mouth and bawled :

' Dare! Come back!'

' Good gracious, he must be deaf! All shout together—now!'

' *Dare !*' they all yelled frantically.

Dare turned slowly round, resting on his rifle.

As if the shout had awakened some unknown power, there was a sudden rushing, scrambling sound, from a bush behind; it parted.

' By the powers! A buffalo!' cried Robin, as a huge beast, shaking his head and snorting, launched himself out of the bush, and with a bound sprang on to the veldt.

' My God, Dare!' said Jack, which was in the thoughts of all.

Rockingham Dare had seen his danger almost as soon as they did.

As the great buffalo caught sight of him he gave a roar, and with distended nostrils began to tear up the ground, pawing and snorting like a demon. Rockingham Dare stood facing him, apparently steady as a rock, as he slowly raised his rifle to the shoulder.

'Pluck enough for a dozen,' muttered Robin; but his voice was very grave.

It seemed a horrid thing to see that slender figure standing opposed to the furious brute, away from cover or escape, his life hanging on the nerve of a moment.

'Now, then!' whispered Jack, in irrepressible excitement, as the buffalo threw up his head and stood for a second stockstill.

Even as he spoke there was a slight snapping crack.

'Missed fire! God help him!' cried Jack.

Dare threw up his hand with a gesture of despair, or it might be farewell, as the buffalo with a stumble and a rush charged straight at him.

Freddy shuddered and turned away; Robin and Jack gazed as if fascinated.

They saw Dare spring aside as the animal reached him, and that the impetus of the brute sent him half a dozen yards beyond. As he passed, Dare flung down his rifle and started wildly running for the tree.

'Poor fellow, he'll never get here!' gasped Jack, as the buffalo, with a sway and a lunge and a roar, turned again.

'It's the only chance,' muttered Robin hoarsely, raising his rifle.

Jack made a half-movement of horror towards him, but with a groan turned away and covered his face with his hands. A wild petition to a Higher Power for his friend's life was all that seemed left to him to do for him now.

'You will *shoot* Dare, I tell you! It is in the line!' cried Freddy, in an agony.

Jack clasped his fingers round his arm like a vice, and forced him to silence.

It is only a flash of time to take a deliberate aim, but it seemed long to them as they held their breath, and their pulses thumped heavily.

Robin's arm was steady, but his face had turned from bronze to pale. A life was in his hand!

One instant, in which there was the flying man, the rushing beast——

Crack! Slow and sullen the report sounded. One second, in which they waited as men wait for doom. Then the smoke cleared.

'Dare is down! The bull's off! You have shot him; I said you would!' screamed Freddy.

'Curse you! My best friend!' said Jack hoarsely, shaken out of all self-control at sight of that recumbent figure on the veldt.

Robin stared as if stupefied, with a look

of rigid horror that made his face as the face of one dead.

'Cain!' he muttered wildly, as he scrambled out of the tree with the others and rushed to the spot.

'Look! look! The bull!' cried Freddy, pointing. 'He is down! he is down!'

'So! How is it?' exclaimed Jack. 'The ball must have passed on. Dare—dear old fellow—can't you speak? Say! Where are you hurt?'

As they bent over him with white, scared faces, what was their astonishment to see him slowly rise to his feet and stagger giddily, his face covered with soil, and great beads of perspiration and blood on his forehead. Then, putting his hand to his head, as if to steady himself, he said, with a dazed smile :

'I am all right.'

'Never! What's this blood?' cried Freddy.

'I came down on a stone.'

'Did you stumble?' asked Jack, mystified still.

'No,' replied Dare. He spoke stiffly and breathlessly. 'Let me rest a moment.'

He gave a gasp for breath ; then, turning to Robin, who stood by with the look of a man who has cast off a burden, he said :

'I saw you were going to fire—at least, I felt it. I knew the danger of my cable being cut by that bullet—or, should you only wound the bull, and he charge. Time to think I had not, but it flashed through me that the ground was my chance ; so, as you aimed, I threw myself down. The fall —going at that pace—has shaken me, I suppose.'

'Give him some liquor—and bless him !' said Jack, smiling broadly, as he pulled out his flask.

'Mr. Adair,' said Rockingham Dare gravely, holding out his hand, 'I owe my life to your presence of mind. It is no exaggeration in this case to say so. I

cannot thank you as I would, but I feel it
deeply. Death, so, is not attractive.'

Robin grasped the extended hand.

'Nonsense! With your ingenuity, I
think I might safely have left you to look
after it yourself. But I congratulate you from
the bottom of my heart on your escape.'

'I gave you up,' said Jack. 'Upon my
soul, I did! And I could ill have spared
you, old fellow. But never mind that, eh?
You have stuck to us, and it's all right.'

But the two friends shook hands with a
glance that said more than words.

'I dare say I did a foolish thing,' remarked Dare, as he gulped down the brandy
and shook the blood from his forehead.

'No,' said Robin. 'The way you kept
your head through the nastiest five minutes
that could befall a man will serve me as a
stock yarn for years. You owe me that,' he
added, laughing, 'for having given me a
shock that will turn me up with heart
disease ten years hence.'

'Nay, it was a near thing. I felt choked,' said Jack, as he passed the flask on to Robin. 'If Mr. Adair had not said he was a pretty good shot, I don't think I could have sat by while he took that aim.'

'I should not have risked it if it had been otherwise,' returned Robin.

'I know!' said Freddy, all his anger turned to admiration. 'You felt as if you'd be a coward if you let Dare be run down; and yet you'd have given some years of your life for the duty to have fallen to some other fellow. I saw it in your face.'

'Don't make me out a hero, Freddy. I assure you I did not feel like one. That bull is dead, or dying! See!'

'Hurrah!' cried Freddy, dancing about. 'We have got his carcase instead of Dare's —ain't I jolly glad? Hurrah!'

'Be quiet, you idiot!' said Jack, with a smile.

'It will be a real fine hide!' said Dare, bending over his enemy.

CHAPTER VI.

LOOKING BACK!

R. CRAIG had an unpleasant duty
to perform ; which, in Irish
parlance, would be termed an
eviction, but which he more simply called
'kicking out a lazy dog of a Kafir.'

He bethought himself of this duty the
day after the party had started for the
buffalo grounds. He found the house a
trifle dull—it seemed so quiet and lifeless.
He had joined Mrs. Dare and Miss Wynyard
on the stoop after breakfast, and endeavoured
to combine conversation with his usual exer-
cise. But as he warmed with his subject,
he had suddenly heard an exclamation from

the latter lady, and soon found himself in
pursuit of a ball of wool down the stoop ;
for how could he refuse to chase it, when
his own flying coat-tails had knocked it off
the bench where it lay. Dear ! What legs
that ball had ! He felt quite blown before
he successfully captured it. After that mis-
chance he walked more gingerly, to avoid
traps of balls and work-baskets ; but it
seemed to him that he had only taken a
few turns again, when he was arrested by a
cry of distress from Mrs. Dare.

' Oh, Mr. Craig, *please* stop ! My *last*
bit of crimson ! Now, if you could only
stand *quite* still for just one minute, I might
unravel you without the silk breaking.'

When Mr. Craig *was* unravelled, he
cheerily remarked that, under the circumstances, he thought they might find his
room more useful than his company ; and,
having ordered round his horse, mounted
and rode away.

It was a hot and dusty ride of some five

or six miles ; and when Mr. Craig reached
the head of the bank that overhung the
clearing where the huts were, he was both
thirsty and tired, and had worked himself
up to a useful state of indignation. The
hut, which had been originally built by
Hottentots, was now inhabited by a Fingo,
and Mr. Craig reflected that he had found
one tenant as profitable, or rather unprofit-
able, as the other.

It was a scene of wild beauty on which
he looked. There were a few green slopes,
a clump of forest-trees with the blended
shades of foliage in which Africa is singu-
larly happy, a belt of flowering mimosa ;
mountains swelling at their base with vivid
greens and browns, and wreathed by a
greyish mist as their lines struck boldly
upwards. One slight peak reared its crown
majestically, as a giant among dwarfs, glittering with the hoar-frost of the night
where it cleaved the snow-line. On red
cliffs near, among bush and mosses, eagles

nested and screamed; and below stood the hut, oblong-built, neutral in hue, but splashed with colour by a crimson weed that meandered its way over the roof, and streaked by green rain-courses adown the blocks of mouldering clay.

Mr. Craig fastened his horse, and descended by a winding path into the sun-baked open space, beaten smooth as a floor with the restless travel of naked feet. The Kafir dogs gave sharp yelling notice of his approach, and the Fingo came out of his hut, and peered round with a majestic air. It changed into a shuffle and an ecstatic grin when he perceived his visitor.

'Hah, Zwartbooy! Good-day to you. Why have you not been up with your rent?'

'I was komen this day, Baas.'

'To bring the rent? Well, I am glad to hear it. As I am here, you may hand it over instead.'

'Baas, I poor man—very poor man; but

it is de troof that I was komen this day to say to the Baas how it was that I have not been able to bring the s'geld.'

' Ah, I thought so! A pretty state of things the country is coming to. Do you fancy you are going to " squat " on my land for nothing ? Simply to give me the pleasure of looking at you. Harkee, Zwart-booy ! You are a lazy, idle, skulking rascal '—and Mr. Craig raised his riding-whip and shook it emphatically at each adjective, and the Kafir instinctively lifted his hand three times as if to ward off a blow—' and if you don't pay up in a week's time, I shall take your cow—your best cow, mind. No lies will serve your turn.'

' Baas,' said the Kafir with a fleeting evil glance, and shrugging his shoulders de-spairingly, ' I have nie " kooes." The cows and the big ox are all my brudder's.'

' Hum !' said Mr. Craig ; ' I thought I had taken your measure pretty correctly. Your brother will pay me a pound a head

27—2

for each of those cattle for the past twelve months, and they will be impounded for trespass until I see the money. And as for you, you humbugging Fingo dog, you will be out of this by this day week—Friday, mark you! I shall send over some one on that day to burn the hut.'

'Baas is cruel to me. I will pay—I have said to the Baas that I will pay ; but it is not my fault that things have gone crooked with me. The veldt is good ; I do not want to leave my house. Will Baas take me on to work it out?'·

'No! I took you on once, and you were not worth your salt.'

At this juncture the Fingo woman, who had been peering round the door listening and cuffing the children into silence, screamed out :

'Oh, it is the big Baas, I see!' and clasping her hands frantically, arrived on the scene, pouring forth exclamations of delight and lamentation, which merged at length into a long string of reasons and excuses, accompanied by passionate gestures.

Mr. Craig listened good-humouredly, but at the end shook his head at the handsome Kafir.

'That will do, Naatje. You have the longest tongue in the valley. You should turn the tap. of it on Zwartbooy, and make him work.'

'The Baas will listen——'

'Nothing of the sort. Why, look ye, Naatje, you get honey enough off the land' —and Mr. Craig pointed to a sack with damp stains that was hanging over a line— 'to pay the rent. You are always selling honey, but the money don't come my way.'

'We eat the honey, Baas ; the poor kinderchies——'

'You must have an almighty big swallow, then. No, I will have no lying, thieving cheats on my land. You ought to be ashamed of yourselves, if you knew what shame meant. That is enough of that. Give me a drink of buttermilk, if you have it—I am thirsty.'

Naatje flew to procure the refreshment, but first brought outside with due pride her solitary chair, and having dusted it conspicuously, set it under a big tree; and Mr. Craig, having carefully tested its staying powers, cautiously sat down.

'Dear me!' he said with a start.

Leaning against a tree-trunk at a little distance was a slip of a girl, in a white frock, with a blue shawl wound round her head, and confining tresses of thick golden hair. She had an abstracted look on her face, but she slowly turned her eyes on Mr. Craig.

'Good-day to you, good-day to you,' he said, nodding to her. He concluded that, being white, if he did not know her he ought to do so.

She made him a slight obeisance, which he thought was a very pretty thing in its way. Then seeing that a sudden crimson flush stained painfully a pair of pale cheeks, he concluded she was shy, and did not speak further to her.

But his eyes kept on wandering that way, for he was puzzled. 'What the deuce was it this girl reminded him of, standing there like that?' How very odd! Suddenly, he never understood how it came to him, he knew. And he drew a sharp quick sigh, and closed his hand nervously, struck by a memory.

The hut had faded, and the copper-coloured children, and the dirty rags blowing in the wind, and the tropical verdure; but the bright sun and the fresh breeze were around him still, and he was back in far-away bonnie Scotland on a summer morning—ah, how many years ago! And the blood was bounding in his young veins with the spirit of hope and adventure, as he lifted his cap off his brown curls and waved it in farewell, and blew kisses back—yes— to Jeanie—his Jeanie—until a turn in the woodland path hid her from his straining gaze. *She* had leant against a tree-trunk and watched him with just that sorrowful look on her face, and she had had golden hair, and a blue shawl framing her fair face. The time had been when he had thought that never while he lived should he forget that picture, and now he had had to cudgel it from his memory ; for he had loved and ridden away, and the dream had faded, like many another when oceans roll between, and ways of life and turns of thought alter. But now, like a dart the thought stabbed him : ' What had become of little Jeanie? Did she break her heart and droop and wither when the lover failed to return as he had promised?'

' *Confound* it !' said Mr. Craig suddenly, as he stroked impatiently his magnificent grey beard. ' How absurd I am ! She is a grizzled old woman by now, thinking about heaven, I suppose, as women do when they get on. This one, now, is thinking about— ribbons, probably, or—*worse.*' He was very angry with himself for that momentary lapse into sentiment. Romancing about buried years might be occupation for a woman's mind; but a man! Psha!

Naatje arrived with the buttermilk just then.

'Have ye got any honeycomb?' he asked, suddenly remembering his own and Mrs. Dare's great partiality for that dainty. 'Ye can send a boy over with it.'

'No, sir,' said Naatje regretfully; 'it is all broked up for the bottles; but Zwart-booy may get you some, perhaps. Miss Dollie,' added Naatje in a low voice, by way of jogging Mr. Craig's memory, and making things pleasant among her guests.

'Miss who do ye say?' asked Mr. Craig, his head appearing out of the can from which he had been taking a long pull.

'Miss Dollie — Haardman,' returned Naatje.

'What, Haardman's daughter, is it?' muttered Mr. Craig, looking across to

where the house glistened whitely about a
mile away. 'Bless me! I should have
known her, of course. But I don't know
that I can call her to mind since she was a
child.'

He put down the can for future attention,
and went up to Dollie, with a cheery 'How
d'ye do—how d'ye do?' and then he shook
hands with her and began to chat.

Dollie's face brightened. It occurred to
Mr. Craig, as she looked shyly up at him,
that if 'Jeanie' had had such starry eyes,
and a smile of that order, perhaps he
might have written oftener, and saved a
'liquor' sometimes to buy a stamp, and
Jeanie might have been his wife years ago.

Dollie did not say much, but she looked
a great deal, and thus conversation
flourished, for Mr. Craig liked a good
listener.

When he returned to his chair and his
buttermilk, Dollie came and sat by him on a
low stool. If Mr. Craig was not the rose,

he was near the rose, and it seemed to Dollie's aching, hungering heart that talking to Jack's father was balm unspeakable to it.

'You asked for honey just now,' she said presently, timidly. 'Naatje gave me a beautiful piece of comb this morning. I wish you would let me send it to Craigmount.'

Her voice was trembling with the bliss of a newly discovered idea. Perhaps Jack would eat some of *her* honey. She could fancy him doing it!

'You are very generous, my child; but I could not deprive you of your honey——'

'It is not generous at all,' interrupted Dollie, with a little smile. 'We care so little for it.'

Mr. Craig then graciously accepted the gift, and Dollie found courage to proffer another request that had been in her mind when she first heard his discussion with Zwartbooy. With some faltering, it was conveyed to him. *Would* he let Zwartbooy stay on? No, not for his sake (hastily)—she knew he was 'schellum'—but for Naatje's. Would he let him have one month to try to pay in? and then—then—well, if he couldn't pay then, Dollie would pay it herself for them. She owed Naatje some money for work as it was, and she would add the rest to it, and thus Naatje would make up the sum.

'What can it signify to you?' asked Mr. Craig, in surprise.

Dollie explained then that Naatje had been their servant until she married, and they were very fond of her. She had really been a good, honest, hard-working girl; and she had had so much trouble since she married with Zwartbooy's lazy ways. And they did not want to leave, and perhaps he might do better now he had had a fright.

'My child,' said Mr. Craig gravely, 'how can you pay a sum of this kind? And, indeed, I could not think of allowing you to dream of such a thing.'

He spoke so decidedly, that Dollie said hurriedly :

'I shall be a—a—rich woman in a month, and I shall have money to pay with—indeed I shall!'

Her face grew scarlet, and two unbidden tears sprang into her eyes, which she turned away to hide.

'Bless me! the girl isn't happy. I wonder what screw's loose,' thought Mr. Craig, who, on these signs of confusion, suddenly remembered that he had heard of her and a coming marriage. He felt sorry for her, he hardly knew why, so he said cheerily and kindly :

'You are going to be married, are you not? Of course, I had forgotten it. Let me wish you every happiness. You will be happy, I am sure. Max Muller, isn't it? A—good fellow,' said Mr. Craig, trying to call to mind which of the brothers it was. 'Good-looking, too,' he added, with airy confidence.

'No,' said Dollie emphatically, in a half-strangled voice.

'No? Well, I am sure he will make you a good husband, and—and—gold, you see, is more lasting than beauty,' said Mr. Craig, as confidently as if he had been sure of the efficacy of his plan of consolation, which he by no means was.

After this there was silence for a while, and Mr. Craig, feeling cooler, bethought him of going. As they rose to say good-bye, Dollie, feeling it was her last opportunity, laid her hand urgently on his arm to prevent his slipping away, and repeated her appeal. He had been so kind, and looked so nice, she did not feel afraid of him at that moment, and she felt brave in Naatje's cause.

Mr. Craig frowned. He could not shake off the childish hand, although he had the wise man's dislike to linger when his mind was made up. He could not for Jeanie's sake. Standing there, meekly pleading, she recalled his lost love almost painfully to him. It had not been the strong fervent love of his manhood, but it had always held in his memory 'the tender grace of a day that is dead,' and the wraith of that little Scottish girl seemed to have risen up at his side to-day.

'You think me foolish to care,' said Dollie, in conclusion; 'but sometimes I have been very unhappy—everyone is, I suppose—and then I have come down here, and Naatje has been kind—and—and talked to me about many things, what she used to do in Natal when she was a girl, and I have almost laughed, until I have forgot my troubles. I have had such happy times under those trees,' added Dollie softly, 'when otherwise I should have been lonely and sad; and I should not like to think of the place without Naatje. Another Kafir might cut them down,' she said, with a shiver.

She did not dare to add what was in her

mind, that under those trees she had often lingered with Jack, while Naatje sat stitching in her hut door.

'Fudge!' muttered Mr. Craig.

But Dollie fancied she saw signs of yielding in his face.

'Is there no place that you have ever cared for like that?' she said more earnestly. 'That you could think of when you were far away? That was like home to you— the best home—because you *loved* it?' And the starry eyes sought his so pleadingly.

'There! *That* will do,' said Mr. Craig most gruffly; but Dollie knew the day was won.

Mr. Craig had always felt thankful to a Providence that had given him no daughters, and at this moment his gratitude was more fervent than usual. Well, he had been wheedled into it, and there was no help for it. Why make the girl wretched for a trifle? Thus, Mr. Craig tried to excuse himself for having yielded to the impulses

of a nature which he would fain believe
was *not* kindly, against some, as he would
have termed them, disastrous instances to
the contrary.

'Well,' he said at length, 'the rascal
shall stay the month, as you seem so un-
accountably set upon it; and at the end of
that—well—well—we'll see ; at least, I'll
see. Don't you worry your head about it.
It will be all right.'

As if by a sudden impulse, he took a
searching look into her face, and smoothed
her soft golden hair back with hands that,
·brown and big and roughened as they
were, were yet shapely and handsome, and
characteristic as John Craig himself had
ever been.

'God bless you, my dear, and your
pretty·face,' he said gravely, with a sort of
gallant grace.

Despite himself, he felt a lurking tenderness for the girl who, however unwittingly,
had brought back to him those golden days

of his youth, when life had looked like a glittering course, and the chariot of Time had not seared the heart with the roll of its leaden wheels.

Then he went hastily away to his horse, only calling out to Zwartbooy, as he passed, to come up to Craigmount on the morrow.

'When a man *does* make a fool of himself,' cogitated Mr. Craig remorsefully, as Punch joggled homewards, '*he goes the whole hog!*'

'I thought he was going to kiss me,' breathed Dollie with parted lips and glistening eyes, and a red flush painting away the wan look on her cheeks. 'If he had—if he had—*Jack's father*—oh, I think I could even marry Max this minute, and feel not to care!'

CHAPTER VII.

RIVAL BEAUTIES.

THE buffalo party were winding through the cliffs that led to the valley late on the following day. The Scotch carts followed, laden with the spoils of war, and their hearts were light as they thought of the comfortable evening before them—perhaps a little of the comfortable beds to follow. Those of the party who were not used to camping out felt knocked up more or less, and they sat their horses wearily.

'I'll be glad to get to my armchair,' remarked Seymour, looking round at the

gathering dusk. 'This horse is not exactly
a — er — rocking - chair. Good gracious!
what's that?' with a jump.

'That? Oh, that's a big baboon,' replied
Jack, with a grin. 'There are echoes here
that make his bark sound fine.'

'Dear me! if you'd said it was a lion, I
shouldn't have been surprised. Brute!
roaring out like that.'

'He is only saying "How-d'ye-do?"' said
Freddy. 'You should hear one with a
tiger knocking at his front door; then there
is something like a shindy.'

'I wonder what will be the next varia-
tion,' grumbled Seymour. 'We have
started out two or three buck already, to
say nothing of hares, and skunks, and meer-
cats by the crowd, and I imagine that is a
tiger purring over there. The veldt seems
alive to-night.'

'Just the night for anything,' said Jack
cheerfully. 'Well,' he added, 'the next
event is that Mr. Steen will say good-

night,' as they came to some cross-roads, and all pulled up.

'Ja. I shall be quick by here. Nacht —so long,' and with congratulations and good wishes they separated.

'Now,' cried Freddy, 'if you are in haste to get home, and we want to blow our trumpets there, let's hurry up.'

Seymour and Robin responded to the invitation and put their horses into a canter, while Jack and Dare pulled up to deliver a joint of meat at a farmhouse they were passing ; a delicate attention that is tolerably sure to be appreciated by South African housekeepers, who labour under many difficulties.

On through the lonely roads went the trio ; the wide open bush veldt now lay around, and the echo of the hoofs was the only sound that broke the stillness. Robin's horse was leading, when suddenly he stopped dead, and threw up his head with a cry—that shrill weird cry of a horse in

fear, that cannot fail to strike the rider with
a sure and sudden sense of danger to come.
It was just the hour when the grey dusk
comes creeping over the veldt, giving to it
such an air of rank desolation, when there
is still a kind of chill yellow light above
the grey, tipping a high bush here and
there with its gleam, and adding what may
be called an infernal glare to streak and
intensify the black shadows of the dreary
plain.

'I see nothing,' said Robin, casting his
eyes along the road and around as the
others drew up behind him.

'There is something, depend,' whispered
Freddy.

Insensibly they lowered their voices as
the sense of the solitariness closed in upon
them, and the cheery sound of their horses'
footfalls died away. At such an hour in a
wild country a man, should he be alone,
instinctively keeps open his eyes and ears,
knowing that if danger there be, it will

surely close in upon him then, and yet that never are his eyes so useless as at this dusk, when the unearthly light casts reflections on every side, and magnifies, reduces, and distorts every familiar object; while the hush that falls tingles on the traveller's nerves with its dreary sense of soundless blank, of a grim yet echoing void. Robin took a 'Derringer' from his breast-pocket, then put it back with a negative shake of the head.

'I wish one knew what to expect,' he said.

A yell rang sudden and shrill across the veldt, and, as if at a given signal, the whole veldt forty yards away seemed to become alive with bounding forms. Each bush gave out its lurking occupant, who sprang into mid-air, vaulting over the bushes around in a series of leaps that recked nothing of the width or height of the obstacle, and seemed only the outcome of a graceful and positive enjoyment of its own strength.

'Wild dogs!' said Freddy sharply. 'But what a pack!'

The leader, with a long-drawn outcry, bounded into the road and crouched down twenty yards in front of them. He stood about as high as an English retriever, having a shaggy light coat with dark splotches on it, and a great square, fierce-looking and hideous head and jowl.

One by one his followers ranged themselves behind him, silently to await his lead, till, perhaps, there were a dozen in the road; but the bush was still alive with the springing shapes of the remainder.

'What a scene for a painter!' muttered Robin, as they sat in their saddles gazing.

The shivering horses; the crouched pack in the road ; the hideous bounding forms leaping in and out over the bush ; the grey stretches of veldt ; the mountains in front with their purple-darkened bases, gaunt sides, and yellowing peaks ; that unearthly glare—and the black-looking sky over all.

'Those bushes must be from seven to ten feet high. What spring the brutes have!'

'They are large-sized,' replied Freddy. 'Had we not better be moving, while they are making up their minds?'

'True,' said Robin. 'I was studying them from an artistic point of view. I forgot their appetites.'

Robin put spurs to his horse, and together they all broke into a gallop.

The leader let them come within a few lengths, as if undecided; then with a yell he swerved off the road, and made away to the right, the whole pack leaping and flying after him.

'Will they follow?' asked Seymour, with his head over his shoulder.

'No; but they must be very fierce to-night,' replied Freddy. 'At one moment I really thought they would have come on— if that leader had just tipped them the wink. Somebody's calves will suffer, I guess.'

'Well, anybody is welcome to my share

of the veldt at this hour,' said Seymour. 'That lurid light shining on those brutes' hideous heads is an "effect" I shall not soon forget.'

'Don't be nervous,' remarked Freddy. 'Wait till you meet with what I did at this time. I was alone one night, leading my horse who had fallen lame, and I came sharp round a bush on a fine pair of tigers quarrelling on a bit of open, close by the roadside.'

'What did you do?' asked Seymour.

'Well,' said Freddy, with a grin, 'I don't think my memory will serve me beyond the fact. Let every man do as he likes under such circumstances, *I* say.'

Glad, indeed, were the wearied travellers when they reached Craigmount. To see its flood of cheery light streaming far out upon the veldt, its willing servants running smiling out to welcome them and take their exhausted horses, gave them a practical illustration once more of the fact 'that there is no place like home.'

And happier still were they when, after a
bath and a ' pick-me-up,' they sat round the
well-spread board and devoured the fatted
calf, with the soft women-faces to kindle and
admire while they made triumphal progress
through their history, and fought their
battles o'er again.

' I am going to say a somewhat profane
thing,' remarked Robin to Jack, as they
sat in lazy enjoyment on the veranda when
supper was a thing of the past.

' Fire away! I am a difficult person to
shock,' was the reply.

' Does not his face'—indicating Dare—
' suggest the " peace that passeth all under-
standing"? Those words have not been
quite Hebrew to me since I knew Rockingham Dare. What a striking expression of
repose ! Either that man is very happy, or
he has been through the furnace, and nothing
can touch him any more.'

' You are fanciful,' replied Jack musingly,
glancing towards where Dare leant against a

honeysuckle-covered pillar near the door, with the light shining full on his face, while he talked to Miss Wynyard, whose dark beauty was set off to perfection by the yellow dress she wore. 'To me he looks much like any other fellow. But I am glad to see him here to-night—more than glad. I shall see him a long time with that buffalo on his heels.'

'Yes, one cannot help thinking of what might have been, on looking at that radiant face.' And Robin turned his eyes on Mrs. Dare. 'She reminds me of some brilliant exotic to-night. So thoroughbred-looking, too—a woman to "grace a court;" and one finds her—here. 'Tis a queer world. There certainly are some very pretty women in South Africa,' he added, with an admiring glance across at Miss Wynyard's perfect profile, at the alabaster shoulders and finely-moulded bust that her square-cut dress revealed. ' Perhaps the last place one would expect to find them.'

'Why should they not be here? They are happy enough,' said Jack stoutly, a little pucker between his brows.

'Mrs. Dare doesn't always look as she is looking to-night,' remarked Freddy, with the air of a connoisseur. 'Do you know'— confidentially—'I have seen her look quite ugly.'

'The fate of many very taking beauties on occasion; but with that beautifully-curved mouth, her bizarre air, and such an unusual pair of eyes, rather difficult to imagine in this case.'

'Fact, nevertheless,' said Freddy sturdily.

'Well, there is one thing—I bet you she did not look — commonplace,' responded Robin, equally decidedly.

'No—o—o; you score there,' replied Freddy. 'But Miss Wynyard is handsomer.'

'Her face is almost perfect, which Mrs. Dare's is not, and her colouring is magnificent. And I have a strong personal preference for dark hair and eyes, as against yellow hair and brown eyes. But, speaking purely as a critic of the two faces, there is one distinction between them.'

'In whose favour ?'

'Mrs. Dare's.'

'Well, what is it ?' said Jack impatiently.

'Nothing much.'

'Give it a name, then.'

'Soul,' replied Robin carelessly, as he moved away to get a light.

'Ah !' said Jack, gazing at Mrs. Dare.

'Seymour calls it "breed,"' remarked Freddy, with a side-glance at his brother. 'I suppose it suits Adair best to call it "soul." Hang "breed," I say! There is more of the other ; she is more alive, too, more flash and strength and—devilishness about her. She don't talk ; but, then, who wants a woman to talk? *I* think Miss Wynyard a deuced sight the handsomer of the two, Jack.'

'Do you ?' said Jack dreamily.

' Yes ; don't you ?' persisted Freddy.

'I cannot admire a woman I dislike,' responded Jack, rousing himself.

' Oh, I am above prejudice of that sort. You think,' Freddy added insinuatingly, ' Mrs. Dare does look most awfully, un- utterably—and all that sort of thing—lovely to-night, eh, Jack?'

' I cannot see anything but the back of her head,' returned Jack carelessly.

' Lord, what a lie !' muttered Freddy.

' What is all that about ? The rival beauties ?' asked Mr. Craig, who had come up behind them with Mr. More unper- ceived.

' Just that,' replied. Freddy.

Jack was too absorbed in striking a match to make any answer.

' I think I never saw a handsomer girl in my life than Miss Wynyard,' said Mr. More, in his deliberate way.

' Ah, yes,' remarked Mr. Craig ; ' very

good-looking women, both of them—an ornament to the house; and I am glad to see them here. When a woman is ornamental, she is fulfilling her mission in the world ; it is when she starts being *useful* that I feel I want to bury her! But let me tell you one thing, that if you were to start those ladies free through the world—and one, I suppose, has eight years on the wrong side of the ledger to her account—that for one fool that fell in love with Miss Wynyard, six fools would fall in love with Mrs. Dare.'

'Now, why?' asked Mr. More. ' I do not say you are not correct. My experience among the ladies has been limited.'

'Difficult to catalogue,' responded Mr. Craig. ' Possibly, because they would all be under the delusion that she was going to fall in love with *them.* Some women *are* like that. And of all the demon wiles with which Beelzebub has endowed the sex, that is perhaps the worst.'

'She looks as if she had plenty of feeling,' adventured **Mr. More.**

'She has got a good many charms, if you begin cataloguing them,' said **Mr. Craig** drily.

Jack turned round in his chair. 'And Miss Wynyard?' he asked.

'Ah, Miss Wynyard,' said **Mr. Craig,** nodding approvingly in that direction. 'Ah, that young lady will always do nicely —nicely—*for herself.* A *head, no heart,* and *never* a scruple! Dear me, a woman in a *thousand!* It used to be my idea that men had heads and women hearts, but I am proud to say I have at last met a woman— Ah, **Mr. Adair,** is that you? What have we to-night? Beautiful weather!—beautiful women!—beautiful scenery! and a well-earned rest! And there are people who can say this world is not a pleasant place!'

'They must be hard to please,' agreed Robin, as he took a turn on the veranda with **Mr. Craig.**

' Look at that melancholy ruin !' muttered
Freddy, pointing to Seymour---' that *thinks*
he's happy.'

' Seymour?' asked Jack.

' Who else? A good old fellow, six feet
six long, and not an ambition in life but to
turn himself into a handy Billy for his idol!
Worse than that, he'd yearn to be a door-
scraper, a door-mat——'

' Chut !' said Jack.

'.There is only one comfort,' grumbled
Freddy. ' When you see a fellow making
that sort of sinful waste of himself over a
woman, you think of *how* he will go in
some day—for something worth going in
for !'

Mrs. Dare and Lucas Seymour were sitting in two easy-chairs placed down the
veranda, with their backs to the speakers.
He was lying back, with a cushion under
his head, and an extinct cigar between his
fingers, looking fixedly at her fair face,
whose bright loveliness was luring him on

to an infatuation his eyes betrayed. In the light that flashed from the windows on her beauty, she looked, as Robin had said, like an exotic with its burning heart, its gorgeous hues ; and yet withal there was a delicacy of colouring, a refinement of form, a softness of manner that removed her charms from that order compelling admiration, and placed them on the list of those that invite it. A subtle difference, in which lies a potent charm, as men have sometimes discovered — to their undoing. She was clothed in softly-falling, black, transparent raiment, through which her snow-white arms and shoulders gleamed, and a scarlet cactus flamed on her breast, and another in her glistening hair. Her great dark eyes burned and flashed, and the pale pink flush the evening air had brought to her cheeks seemed to waver with each breath under her transparent skin. She idly waved a huge black fan, while she talked in low sweet tones.

29—2

'Listen to them,' said Freddy, in a low voice to Robin, who had joined them again; 'it is real fun to hear how old Seymour comes out when he is talking to her. He who used not to have one word to knock against another, he will talk the most wonderful bosh. Listen!'

'I know what he would like to say,' replied Robin, with a smile; 'but I don't suppose he is saying that.'

Mrs. Dare's voice rose upon the silence.

'Yes, that is true. A great deal of the writing nowadays brings to mind the brevity and pithiness of the glorious old Bible style. Contrast the books and articles of the present day with the past. No long-winded sentences; no elaborate and elegant phrasing; no speeches that work up so gracefully if tediously to their point. We have impassioned oratory, it is true, but it is in the knock-and-hammer style; like our conversation, curt and incisive. Ah, it is an age of condensing, is it not? Everything falls a prey to it—the fashionable orator no more exempt than the—milk!'

'Go it, fair lady!' muttered Freddy. 'That might stump *some* fellows! A month ago, Seymour would have said, 'Hey?' and got no further.

'Just that. Multum in parvo. We live at railroad speed, and it creeps into every-thing. We have more amusements and distractions in a day than our forefathers had in a month, and yet in the result we are always bored and craving, and early worn out. The truth is, Mrs. Dare, the pull on men's brains in these rapid days destroys their bodies, so to speak. We have no longer the sort of animal vitality the old blokes had, that let them enjoy what-ever turned up.'

'Robin!'

Miss Wynyard's clear tones summoned her lover to her side. Laying down his pipe, he went to her.

'You called me?' he said interrogatively.

'If I had not, I do not for a moment suppose that you would be here,' she replied, her eyes darkening with anger.

'I thought that you were talking to Mr. Dare,' he answered somewhat carelessly.

'Mr. Dare is a very pleasant man; I wish you could give yourself the trouble to take a leaf out of his book. However, as Mr. Dare and I are not to pass our lives together, is it unreasonable that I should expect occasionally to be favoured with your society as well as his?' she asked sarcastically.

Miss Wynyard's manner was cold and overbearing, and Robin, who might be led with a silken thread by those he loved, but was somewhat impracticable to drive, answered with a slight shrug of the shoulders and a coldness that overmatched her own :

'Perhaps, as we *are* to do so, it is of less consequence how much of them we spend in each other's company now. What did you call me for? Anything I can do for you?'

'I wanted to show you the bracelet you ordered for me from England, that came while you were away; but as after an absence of three days you have not yet cared to join me for five minutes, I conclude you are without interest in what concerns me.'

Robin frowned uneasily. Had he been discourteous? Yes, truly — unwittingly. Having lashed himself with a short self-examination, he bent forward, and drew Miss Wynyard's arm through his, and led her to the farther end of the veranda.

'Do not let us quarrel about a trifle of this sort, Julia,' he said in his usual gentle tones. 'For my society, simply, I am bound to say you have not hitherto shown any special desire. If you think that I have not paid you sufficient attention in the eyes of the world, I hope you will forgive me. I will endeavour to make amends.'

An angry retort rose to Miss Wynyard's lips, but prudence controlled it; she saw that never had her hold upon Robin been less than it was at this moment. Could she tell that while away from her and camping under the quiet stars at night, he had allowed himself the intoxicating draught of thinking much of his lost love, and that to take up his weary chains again, seemed like a fresh infidelity to that dear memory?

'What a speech for a lover!' she said scornfully.

'We are hardly ordinary lovers,' returned Robin quietly. 'When I asked you to honour me with your hand I made few protestations, as you may remember, and you said that you neither desired nor expected them—or to that effect. I knew you would accept me when I asked you, Julia; but I hardly deceived myself into thinking it would be because you cared for me. I thought we understood each other.'

A flush rose to Miss Wynyard's forehead.

'Did you expect me to care for you when you did not care for me?' she asked, half passionately.

'No, I did not,' replied Robin tranquilly.

She skilfully changed the ground of attack.

'You are not to all women as you are to me. I have seen you linger in Mrs. Dare's company hour after hour, looking at her admiringly, talking to her gaily, brightly, as if it were a pleasure to converse with her. Do you think her very handsome?'

'Very lovely—yes.'

'You admire her more than me, then? Is that why you seek her society?'

Robin hesitated, while a look of impatience swept over his face, and the lines of his mouth hardened.

'That is true, then?' she said haughtily.

He answered hurriedly, impatiently:

'Your beauty is unquestionable. I do not imagine I am the first to tell you so.

As to Mrs. Dare, I have been used to that style of woman all my life; she is like a breath of home air to me. I suppose that is why I get on with her.'

'That is almost an insult to me. Do you mean it so?' asked Miss Wynyard, a sombre fire creeping into her eyes.

'Do not take it, as I did not intend it. I merely meant that having been brought up, as it were, on the same lines, we have many ideas and sentiments in common.'

'Which we have not.'

'I must agree with you.' Robin spoke with deeper impatience. 'If you were only content to ignore mine—as a rule you go out of your way to trample on them. Pardon me if I am unjust, but it seems like it.'

'Do you expect me to be a nonentity, simply to reflect your opinions?'

'Far from it. If you think I am a man capable of setting up a standard, you misjudge me yet a little more than you have done throughout, to-night.'

'Robin,' she said, coming suddenly closer to him and laying her hand on his arm, 'if I knew you cared for me I might, perhaps, be different in many things.'

Was the coldness that had been her attraction for him going to fall from her like a mantle? Robin shuddered.

'You are a stone, I believe!' she exclaimed vehemently.

'I hope not,' he replied, taking her hand. 'Such as I am, I trust you will overlook my faults, and make the best of me. If you regret——'

'No; I do not regret,' she interrupted hastily. 'You have said I am beautiful. What is there in me that a man cannot love?'

She asked the question half proudly, with the moonlight shining down on her beautiful face, with its setting of lustrous coils of jetty hair, on her perfect shoulders, on her snowy arms.

'Many men would love you madly—
believe it. It is your royal right. That
I have no love to give'—he paused with
his eyes averted, then added hastily—
'should be a source of regret to me in this
case.'

'Is it?' she asked; her face, as it seemed
to him, passion-shaken, her voice sweet
and low, in itself a caress.

He passed his arm round her and drew
her to his breast—those perfect lips were
very close to his——

'Yes,' he murmured, laying his own
lightly on them.

Hers clung eagerly, passionately to his;
then her eyes were lifted to his darkened,
bewilderingly sweet.

'Will you be always to me thus—cold
in all the days to come?' she asked softly.

She was a beautiful woman pleading for
his love with all the gentleness that was
a sure attraction to a man of his stamp.
He was a gallant English gentleman—she,

his promised wife. The ground was being cut from under his feet, and he knew it! It was the old, old story of the tempter and the tempted, only here the temptation was so slight.

'Why try to pry into the future?' he asked gently.

'Tell me,' she said.

'Dear, when you are mine I will try to make your life happy—that you shall have no wish unfulfilled.'

'Tell me,' she repeated softly again, while her head rested in abandonment on his breast. 'If you mean "Yes," put me from you ; if you mean "No"——'

'No,' he whispered with sudden fervour, and she won from him the first lover's kiss he had ever given her.

When she had left him, he wandered out into the darkness away from the lighted veranda. Long he paced up and down under the quiet starlight.

'God, how I hate myself and her !' he

muttered at last, as he turned towards the house.

'I shall win!' said Miss Wynyard victoriously, as she looked at her own reflection in the looking-glass that night. 'And he is very handsome. The world shall not be able to say that the man I am going to marry does not care two straws about me!'

*   *   *   *   *   *

'I must be off at daylight to-morrow,' remarked Rockingham Dare to Jack, as they stood in the dining-room drinking whisky-and-water. 'I have been away four days; and with Clarke away too, I shall find the farm gone to the deuce.'

'Cannot you get over for our picnic?'

'In two days? Impossible. If I can make time I will ride over in the evening, and see how you have enjoyed yourselves.'

'You stay here for the picnic, don't you?' asked Seymour anxiously of his fair companion on the veranda outside.

'Yes, indeed; Mrs. Craig has asked me.

Picnics don't fall to our lot every day, you know.'

' I wanted you to be at this one,' he said, bending forward with sudden earnestness, ' because—because it is my last.'

' How so ?'

' No one knows it yet,' he replied, with his eyes fixed on her face, ' but I am going to leave the colony.'

' For good ?' she asked in surprise. ' I thought you were a fixture.'

' So did I. Nevertheless, I find it expedient to go.'

Still the same unwavering gaze—almost a hungering look, it seemed. Then she turned round, lifted her eyes, and his dropped.

' This is a sudden resolution, is it not ?'

' I cannot deny it.'

She looked down again, and quietly folded her fan and rose.

' I am sorry,' she said gently; ' but of course you know your own affairs best.'

'I would rather have won those words from your lips than gained the Victoria Cross,' he said eagerly.

'Surely they are not unnatural to our *friend,*' she said, with a sweet lingering smile.

'Rock,' said Mrs. Dare to her husband, as they stood together in the deserted dining-room, while the gentlemen smoked their good-night cigars on the veranda, 'what was that Freddy was saying to-night about you and Mr. Adair and the buffaloes? He stopped suddenly when he saw me—tell me what it was?'

'Oh, nothing important.'

'You did not wish me to know!'

'It will only worry you next time I go out.'

'No, it won't. I shall be more anxious if you don't tell me the truth.'

Thus adjured, Dare gave a hasty sketch of his adventures.

'Rock, my darling,' she said gravely when he had finished, while the tears stood in her eyes, 'I shall indeed say "Thank God" when I say my prayers to-night, and as long as I live I shall say "Bless Mr. Adair" somewhere in them!'

'And *I*,' he returned passionately, as her soft lips touched his cheek, 'have never ceased, since the day I first saw you, to say "*Thank God!*"'

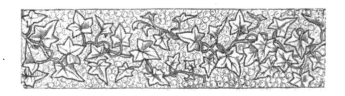

CHAPTER VIII.

A PICNIC.

 'DAY made on purpose !' remarked Seymour with gusto, as
he stretched his long legs on
the veranda and gave a prodigious yawn.

'Hooray for our picnic !' cried Freddy,
who had just arrived in flannels from the
river. 'Tell you what it is, old fellow,' he
added, eying Seymour thoughtfully, 'you
are going clean to the deuce—I am sure you
are, and I'm blowed if I know who is to
stop you! Here you are, up the first in the
morning—you who used to *live* in your bed
—and you have got soft all over, like a
rolypoly pudding ; and you're awfully

thoughtful and contented, and deucedly civil and obliging to everyone ; in fact——'

'Something rotten in the state of Denmark, eh ?'

'I don't know whether Denmark ever got into the fix you're in ; but if she had, and she belonged to me, I should have been dashed uneasy about her. I *do* feel uneasy,' continued Freddy, ' because I have known fellows get like you—and go to heaven.'

' *Heaven !* Well, I should think that is the one place where my friends might give up being uneasy about me.'

'Heaven is a long way off,' remarked Freddy thoughtfully. ' And I always think it will be lonely. One will meet so few fellows one knows.'

' Well, you will know where to find 'em anyway if you miss 'em,' suggested Seymour. ' Now, here fellows are always dropping in and out at inconvenient seasons. You go to China and onwards after a fellow it is a matter of life and death to you to

30—2

see—can you come up with him ?   No such
luck !   If you can do nothing else, you will
go in at one end of a station as he goes out
at the other.   But *count* upon a man's
absence—see him on board a P. and O., if
you like it—and go and borrow his signa-
ture, or his wife, or anything else you think
may come in handy while he has no use for
it, and if you don't run up against him next
day in Bond Street, you *may eat your hat!*'

'This darned world,' said Freddy solemnly,
'is a thing you can neither stick to nor leave
without unpleasantness!'

'Well, it has got its best side uppermost
to-day, the gods be praised!' said Seymour,
putting a starry, scented Mandevillea in his
coat, and looking out to where the hills
flushed a soft pink in the clear, silent
African dawn.

'A morning on which one feels as fresh
as paint,' remarked Freddy, with an appre-
ciatory sniff at the cool air.   'Ever seen a
sunrise before ?'

'No; but I always meant to take a look at one.'

'You will enjoy it then,' suggested Freddy gravely.

'Far from it. It is one of those unpleasantnesses, like the British Museum, you are expected to know about. People think it odd you have never chanced on one — strangers, I mean.'

'Possibly.'

'*I* think a sunrise is—er—indelicate. As a subject of conversation, I mean. Unless you are an astronomer or labourer, you *can* only see sunrises by a habit of being out of bed at — er — improper hours——'

'Hallo, Seymour!' exclaimed Robin's cheery voice. 'Not been to bed yet?'

'Ha!' said Freddy, 'I thought it would give you a shock to see him.'

'Well, it looked a jolly day, our picnic was coming off, and I thought I'd get up, and make up my mind to enjoy life. I had

not forgot the early bird and the worm,'
replied Seymour.

'Ah!' said Freddy, 'there are " worms "
and " worms," and history don't tell which
kind of worm that was. Now, if *I* ever got
up early, resolved to begin enjoying myself, I came a cropper before the day was
out—guv'nor came, or something!'

Three hours later they had all started for
the picnic ground. Jack drove Mrs. Dare
in his 'spider,' Freddy and Mr. Helmsley
rode, and the others patronized the waggon
—a waggon provided with mattresses, comfortable cushions, and a large white cover-
ing that was spacious enough to convey the
party, though augmented by two young
ladies and their brother from a neighbouring
farm.

Away they went, keeping to the road at
first, then striking across country on faint
tracks where the veldt was open, and pick-
ing up the road again as they neared the
hills. Through the dewy flower-studded

veldt they passed on into the mountainous region, and into the cool dark gorges that intersected it, where flourished many an ancient bit of forest that might have been untrodden by the foot of man, but where the monkeys held high revelry among the clinging parasites, and the honeysucker, like an animate jewel, flashed around the tree-blossoms.

'Been here before?' asked Mrs. Dare of Jack doubtfully, as they drew up on a river's bank which lay in their road to ford before they could continue their journey.

'Ay, several times,' he said cheerfully; 'and we will give that lumbering old waggon a lead. It looks deep, but it isn't so, very; although, I remember, it has a mortal bad bottom. Look after your skirts and catch hold of me, if you think you are going. Ready? Fire away, my lads!' And Jack whipped up his pair of greys, and with a grind and a splash they were in the water.

It *was* deep. .The water splashed up over

the animals' backs and soon rose to the axles of the wheels, while the horses stepped delicately and suspiciously, as if they had great doubts of the wisdom of the course they were pursuing.

'I say,' said Jack, when they had got about a third of the way across, 'I did not expect this; I hope the horses will be able to keep their feet. There is a hole somewhere, but I don't fancy it is hereabouts. Well! here we are, and we can't get back now, so we may as well drive ahead. Mind, hold to me, whatever comes. Don't be frightened—there is nothing to be frightened at. We'll get over, by good luck.'

'No, I am not frightened,' said Mrs. Dare somewhat piteously, clinging on to the rail at the back, and a piece of Jack's coat. 'But I *wish* it would not get any deeper.'

'No use to wish that,' responded Jack cheerfully. 'It's bound to get deeper.'

Mrs. Dare did not attempt any further

remonstrance ; even if the rocks and stones
over which they were clambering, to fall
down with a jerk and a sullen splash the
other side, had left her any breath for the
purpose, her experience had taught her that
it is much too late for regrets or change of
purpose when you find yourself with your
charioteer in mid-stream in South Africa.
To turn back from anything in which he is
embarked is not an Englishman's manner,
and in the colony he grows more dogged
and daring than at home. *Never*, unless
your internal machinery and your nerves
are of cast-iron, put yourself without re-
serve into the hands of a born colonial.
He will break every bone in your body,
kill you if necessary, sooner than ' take his
hand from the plough ;' and will stand later
alongside the couch where you repose your
broken bones, and, after the proper con-
dolences, will airily remark : ' By Jove!
Can't think to this day how it happened.
Been over that bit of ground half a dozen

times since, and everything as right as a trivet!' You feebly remark that the 'rains' were at the bottom of the mischief, that they had rendered the road on that particular occasion 'impassable.' 'Ah, yes, hang it!' he will say; 'but I *could* not know that before I started, could I?' He smiles indulgently at the term 'impassable.' It has a foreign sound to him. The word may be in your dictionary; it is not in his.

Neither Jack nor Mrs. Dare paid their lives or bones as the forfeit in this case. When the horses had scrambled up in a cat-like fashion on the opposite bank, which was of sand, and almost perpendicular, and stopped to breathe, Jack turned round and gave a look over his companion.

'How are you—wet?' he said sadly. 'That is a real nuisance. I thought you would keep your feet up out of the water.'

'Oh, Jack, never mind my dress, never mind my boots—I have got my *life!*' cried Mrs. Dare enthusiastically.

Jack smiled.

'Let us see the others hold on to theirs,' he said.

And they sat down on the bank, waving their handkerchiefs in encouragement. The riders followed steadily, throwing their feet out of the stirrups and tucking their legs well up to keep them dry; but the waggon stuck for awhile in mid-stream, as the foremost oxen considered it imprudent to go on, and, jerking themselves free of their leader, turned round with their faces to their comrades, and their tails to the way they should go.

This is a trifling occurrence, however, as things go in South Africa, which the Kafir drivers proceeded to set right by such an amount of cursing and yelling and thrashing as would suffice to keep a horse moving from John o'Groat's to Land's End! To fight with a refractory ox in a strong stream successfully, requires you to have served your apprenticeship to the profession;

also that you may know when·he is likely
to lie down; and further, when you should
harness another team to him to drag him
out, lest the current should become too
strong for waggon and cattle.

'What brutes they are!' said Jack placidly
from the bank, while the notes of Seymour's
cornet floated in wailing remonstrance across
the river to the tune of 'There is Nae
Luck.'

'Yes,' replied Mrs. Dare. 'Klaas told
me that once on a trip they had an ox
that would lie down, and nothing would
get him up. He found it answered; so
one day he did it when they had just started,
and at last they had to light a fire under
him—even then he did not hurry.'

'Now we're away!' cried Jack, making
for the spider, as the drivers' whoops grew
frantic, and the oxen, with a lunge and a
rush and a terrific splashing, tore through
the stream and scaled the bank. 'Always
take an ox while he is in the mind for it!'

The ground they had selected for the picnic was a beautiful sloping piece of turf on the side ·of a small rise, overshadowed by the yellow-wood and stink-wood trees; down below trickled a small stream with the willow on its banks, and the thorny acacia dotted the veldt around.

The ladies were thankful to rest in the shade and unpack, while the Kafirs collected wood and made fires. There were kettles to be boiled, and vegetables to be cooked, and everyone was anxious, at first, to take a share of the fun, and cook what he or she believed to be her strong point ; but soon the heat and smoke of the fires, and the upsetting of saucepans, abated their ardour, and they strolled away to explore, leaving the Kafirs in possession of the kitchen.

Mrs. Craig and Mrs. Dare made a collection of beautiful maiden-hair ferns that grew amongst the stones and crevices of the rock, and Miss Helmsley, escorted by

Jack, came back laden with the purple
lotus blooms, to find Robin and Miss
Wynyard fighting with the table-cloth, and
Freddy adding to their difficulties by pelt-
ing them with leaves and bits of stick from
where he wriggled on the top of a tall
sapling, that swayed with him in the wind
like that uncanny cradle of nursery lore.
Seymour had obligingly consented to lie
on his back and hold on to a corner of the
table-cloth, for the defeat of the ' wandering
breezes,' and Mr. Helmsley held a raving
dog in each hand to ensure the safety of
the larder.

Bottles of honey and cream and trifles in
big jars, jam-puffs, fruits, and salads, with
fowls, ducks, sandwiches, and hard-boiled
eggs for solids, formed the materials for
the feast : a banquet over which the forest
giants spread their branches, while the sunlight struck across the bright dresses, and
on the clumps of a dark-leaved bush with
roseate trumpet-flowers and coming fruit,

that formed a tropical-looking background. Later the ladies were toasted, and speeches made very much to the purpose, amid the cheers and jokes of the audience ; and, after a duet from Mrs. Dare and Seymour, which sounded exceedingly impressive in the solitude of the forest, and struck the dogs with envy till they howled again, Jack rose, with a tumbler of champagne in his hand, and solemnly gave one last toast :

' Ladies and gentlemen, I need not ask your support for this ever popular toast. I am sure it is a *tender* point with you, and I believe I shall find that your feelings are at one with my own when I propose, " *The Colony and its Roads for ever !*" '

' I am going for a walk,' remarked Mrs. Dare, gathering up her white dress and setting her hat firmly on her head.

' For a scramble, you mean,' responded Jack, from the mossy bank where he lay fanning himself with his hat, and muttering

at intervals, ' Deuced hot!' ' A walking-
stick and no beau,' he added. ' You are not
half-equipped, Mrs. Dare.'

' Beaux are all asleep,' she returned, ' and
I feel quite independent of them. If you
hear me scream, you can come, or send some
one.'

' I think it will save me trouble in the
long-run to come now,' said Jack. ' Let us
take this turn—down to the river. There is
a fine bit of cliff away there that I know
you will admire, and you wanted some lotus.'

They trod their way carefully through
the trees and acacia, then on to the bush-
dotted slopes that led to the river.

' How superb Miss Wynyard is looking
to-day in that Gainsborough hat!' said Mrs.
Dare, as she strayed about filling her hands
with jasmine and wild clematis.

' Oh, that is a Gainsborough, is it?' replied Jack, as he held down a high branch
for her. ' I noticed the feathers were
" superb "—not " Cape," though.'

'Barbary, I think. But if the feathers are beautiful, what of the face ?'

' I'll take the feathers,' said Jack, laughing. ' I should as soon think of being in love with a tiger. Do you think it will " do " for Adair ?'

' Yes,' she replied, with a smile ; ' at least, he is getting fascinated, I think. That may not be love, though. I should have thought Mr. Adair was a man who would care very deeply and truly, if at all.'

' Yes, I suppose it would be worth a woman's while to have a fellow like that in love with her. He need not have thrown himself away on that girl.'

' She is beautiful.'

' A man wants something besides beauty to wear through a lifetime,' remarked Jack. ' 'Tis but a fading flower. Am I ungallant to allude to such a subject ?'

' Not the least ; you and I always live in a palace of truth. And I quite agree that Mr. Adair is just the sort of man to fall a prey to a woman who will not make him happy. Clever men are so often wanting in hard, everyday common-sense. It is the doctrine of compensation, I suppose.'

'There is nothing more destructive to common-sense than a woman, you know,' suggested Jack.

'So I imagine ; but I do not know why the common-sense in the beginning should not choose the woman that is to be so.'

Jack laughed..

'Women have put us on the shelf in that as in other matters.'

'Look !' said Mrs. Dare suddenly. 'Don't be startled. Look below !'

Jack looked in silence.

They stood on a shelf of rock overhanging the river, with a winding path leading down to where it formed a shallow bay, away from the deeper current. In the pool were big stones moss-grown, and a Kafir woman standing washing ; on the banks, under the shadow of a wild chestnut dipping its leaves towards the water, a young girl sitting resting her head on her hand, two brown babies rolling on a blanket, and a saddled pony nibbling the grass near them.

'It is Dollie,' muttered Jack presently, in a constrained voice.

'I know it,' said Mrs. Dare gently. 'Rock and I met her yesterday. But how strange—here!'

'This country lies at the back of their farm, some two miles. Only it is a long round to us. Let us go,' added Jack abruptly, averting his eyes from the figures at their feet.

But one brown baby set up a yell as the deeper tones reached them, and the Kafir woman looked up with a start. 'Look, Missie!' she said sharply.

Dollie raised her head wearily, and saw the two figures above her, then sprang to her feet with the colour flushing her face. Jack gravely lifted his hat as she gazed up at him with parted lips.

31—2

Poor Jack! He was struggling with his emotion, that his companion should not see it, striving to thrust it behind him for his own sake. Sometimes the painful thought had been with him that perhaps Dollie had never really cared, that she was taking with contentment to her new life, that he had no hold on her memory. He would try to wish that it might be so in the future, for her sake ; but oh, that the past should have been hollow—unreal! One glance at her upturned face revealed the truth, and the joy was crueller than the pain had been. Where were the flower and the brilliance of her beauty gone? Jack dug his heel into the earth fiercely.

' Poor girl, how ill she looks !' murmured Mrs. Dare, with womanly sympathy.

Dollie bowed her head, then turned away with a movement of dejection that struck home to Jack's heart.

' I must speak to her, or she will think me a brute,' he said unwillingly and harshly, as if in revolt against himself. Mrs. Dare nodded, and turned away on the backward path. 'Don't leave me,' said Jack sharply, springing in front of her, and laying his hand on her arm.

'Why?' she asked gently. 'I shall go slowly and rest—you can overtake me if you like. You would rather be alone.'

'Stay!' said Jack imperatively. 'You must! I dare not be left alone—as things are, I dare not. Look here!' he continued fiercely. 'I have fought with this—believe me, I have tried to live it down. If I let myself go, I shall have it all over again—all, or I dare not answer for the consequences. Away from her I can bear the pain—somehow, I don't want to be a false hound ; but, O God, when I see her I am not master of myself! When I think that she is not mine—that she never will be mine—I feel that I must go to the ends of the earth to avoid her.'

With a fierce rush the words came from

his trembling lips with such a force of pent-up pain as must have moved a heart of stone.

'Jack, dear Jack!' said Mrs. Dare, feeling a sudden big lump in her throat. It was all she said, but she turned round by his side.

Together they scrambled down the narrow path, and Dollie rose as they approached. With a winning smile, Mrs. Dare held out her hand.

'How d'ye do? What a pretty spot you have chosen for a rest! Mr. Craig and I were taking a walk, and stumbled upon it by accident ; but it is fortunate for me, for I have been wanting to see Ketka for some time about washing. So I will go and speak to her now, and see how her views and mine agree.'

Dollie murmured something indistinct, and Mrs. Dare, pleased at having got herself so comfortably out of a difficulty, gathered up her dress and, stepping carefully from stone to stone, at last reached Ketka in the water, and poised herself on a broad slab of granite, where she might discuss matters with the Kafir out of earshot of Jack and Dollie.

'I never thought of giving Ketka my washing,' cogitated Mrs. Dare ruefully ; 'but now I suppose I am in for it.'

Ketka was all smiles ; her brown fingers had long been itching to manipulate those numberless white dresses which made Mrs. Dare's 'wasch clothes' such a fortune to the lucky girl who could secure them. With this in her mind, she had hastily dropped the big stone with which she had been scrubbing the unfortunate garments, and, when Mrs. Dare landed by her side, she found the linen spread on a smooth stone like a table, and Ketka slowly rolling the lather up and down on it with the palm of her hand.

'Daag, Missis,' said Ketka sweetly, not forgetting to drop the soap behind her, that she might steal a glance to ascertain how matters were progressing with Jack and Dollie.

'What can I say to you, Dollie?' asked Jack. He had not taken her hand—he seemed to have forgotten it—but his eyes were eagerly and covetously devouring her face.

She stood in front of him, her fingers tightly locked together, and the haggard lines of trouble, so apparent in the pitiless African· sunshine, defacing the youth and beauty of her face.

'Nothing,' she said passionately, raising her eyes to his full of unshed tears. 'I wish—I wish—I was dead!'

'Don't,' he said gravely. 'I have tried not to wish that for myself; it hurts me to hear you say so.'

At the enforced calmness of his voice the tears dried up, and her eyes grew bright.

'If you cared for me,' she exclaimed

fiercely, carried away by the swift tide of her own pain, ' if you cared, as you have said, you would rather see me dead—dead at your feet—than give me—up to— Max !'

' If I cared !' Jack shivered as if he had received a blow. ' Yes, Dollie,' he said, still gently. ' If . I had loved you—as a savage—selfishly—that might have been my instinct. It is natural in its way. But that is not the kind of love I have given to you, dear. I have held you before myself—always !'

Dollie's lips quivered, but she answered nothing.

' What is it ?' he asked at last, as she stood looking on the ground. ' What is amiss ? You said just now, " *if* you cared." Can you dare to say that you think I do not care ? Look at me, Dollie, and say that you never thought such a lie.'

But Dollie looked away from him, while two big tears coursed down her cheeks.

There was a yearning sound in Jack's voice when he spoke again.

'I have suffered—God knows! do not you doubt it.'

There was no reply; only the strange look on her white face deepened. His self-control was slipping from him, but he would hold to it while he might.

'What have I done?' he said determinedly, coming nearer to her. 'Is it my fault—any of it? What do you doubt me for? Did *I* leave *you?* Can you reproach me that I left any stone unturned to win you? Ah! in those weary days and nights, and again when I saw your face to-day, I felt you know not what agony of remorse for all I *had* done to win you. Why did I not leave my flower as she lives in my memory that night I first saw her? As it was to end so, I have wished it for you—for myself, *never, never!'*

Jack's voice was vibrating with deep passion now.

' I would give my life to undo the past—that may not be ; but my love you have had in as full measure as man can give to woman. How you can doubt it—if you do—I know not.'

He looked away over the hills, and his usually keen eyes were almost misty. When he again broke the silence, he spoke dreamily, as if more in answer to his own thoughts than to her :

' Did I not go to the verge of dishonour —murder, for you ? and, if you had bidden me, I should have gone beyond. I should have tried not, but it would have come so; I was a plaything in your hands. My God! I am nothing else now !'

Slowly Dollie raised her eyes to his with a long, inquiring look.

' It is easy to say those things—when you are with me,' she said.

Jack looked at her for a moment as if struck dumb ; then, with a groan, turned aside. He took a few steps

away, then turned, and came quickly up
to her.

'I will go,' he said shakily. 'If I stayed
here, I should crush that lie down your
throat with my kisses. The girl *I* loved I
have lost to-day. There is nothing for me
to wait for.'

He moved away slowly, and climbed the
bank behind them. But he had hardly
reached the top and turned off among the
trees, when flying footsteps came behind
him.

'Jack!' called Dollie breathlessly—'Jack!'
He stopped unwillingly.

'Let me go,' he said. 'Can you not leave
me alone—leave me to my misery?'

'Do not go so,' she pleaded, seizing his
hand.

He withdrew it gently.

'Jack,' she said lovingly, while she crept
to his side with the tears chasing each other
swiftly down her cheeks, 'do not let me
remember you like this—harsh and cruel.

You have never been that to me. It is the last time, Jack—and we *have* cared.'

' *Have* cared!' he muttered. ' Dollie— little love—don't cry !'

His voice took the old tenderness with the last words, and then she broke down utterly.

' My darling, *don't!*' said Jack imploringly. ' You will drive me—I don't know where. I thought you did not care, or something, and I had better go quick. You know a man does not bear torture as well as a woman,' he added, with a faint smile, ' so he is best out of it—sharp !'

' Jack, I *did* care ; that was what made me say those things to you.'

' Eh ?'

' I was so *glad* when I saw you—that I hated myself for it. They told me—oh, Jack !—that you did not care now—that— you—were—happy.'

' *Damn* them ! whoever " they " may be,' said Jack emphatically.

' It is not true ?'

' No, false as hell ! I believe it never will be true,' he said blankly.

' Jack, do not you think *I* have suffered ?'

He looked down at the childish face that had lost its colour and roundness, that wore that weary stricken look of abiding sorrow, and a pang of pain shot across his own.

' I am afraid so, my darling—God forgive me !'

' You,' she said wearily, while the tears trembled in her voice—' you can suffer perhaps, but not always—pain lies dead sometimes—numb and quiet. Then you can have peace ; for it is like peace—it comes hard, and it goes quick, but it is there. *I* suffer—*always*. When my peace comes, it is driven from me. You are free, but *I*,' she added passionately, ' am *bound*. To love you—and yet to be in bondage ! to have another's touch, another's kisses, while my heart cries for you. Ah, in my loathing and my shame, I do wish I were dead.

Perhaps God will hear some day, and take me — it is better to die, than to live so.'

As the picturesque passionate words broke from her lips, Jack shivered in the hot sunshine.

' Cease !' he said in a low strained tone. ' Cease—for pity's sake ! There are things that turn a man into a devil. Do you think that I do not——'

He broke off as he buried his face on her arm.

' Now go,' said Dollie gently, at last. ' Go, dear Jack. It would have broken my heart to let you go so—but now——'

He lifted his head and looked at her. A long look.

' Come here,' he said, holding out his arms, ' once more—you must.'

He drew her into them, and his voice quivered with triumph.

' Why did you care for my *life*—that day ? Go ! it is easy to say, but if I elect to

stay. Who is to make me go? I think—
Dollie—I shall—*never*—go.'

'Yes—you—will,' she said, with an ap-
pealing look, her heart beating fearfully—
'you will not *forget*——'.

'Kiss me then!' he said hoarsely. 'Kiss
me—so that I may dream you are *mine*.
Kiss me once—oh, love—and no woman's
lips——'

'Hush!' she said feverishly—'I love you
too well to take your life so.' A slow
radiant light broke over her face. 'But I
know now how you—love—me, and I am
happy—happy. Kiss me, if you will. Ah,
God bless you, *my* Jack!'

Mrs. Dare picked her way back over the
stones, and Ketka stealthily picked up her
discarded stone, and stuck a lump of tobacco
between her shining teeth.

'Ah,' she said, counting on her fingers,
'meal—coffee—sugar—money come with
dat Missis' wasch clothes! Good Missis!
Dutch Missis too wise—he, he! I like

English Missis. A-c-h, what a mooi' (fine) 'country must be England, where all de fools live!'

Mrs. Dare reached the top of the bank, then, hearing a noise, she turned aside to see Dollie leaning against a tree convulsed with sobs. Mrs. Dare went up to her and bent down, imprinting a gentle kiss on her forehead.

'Poor child!' she said pitifully; 'don't cry like that. It is hard, I know—I pity you both from the bottom of my heart; but try not to grieve so, little one. Sometimes when the cloud is blackest the light shines through. Life is not *always* dark—for anyone.'

'You are good and kind—but *no one* can help me,' returned Dollie, with an anguished look.

'No one *here*,' said Mrs. Dare, with gentle emphasis; 'but somewhere there is help, Dollie. May it come to you, and make you happy—some day!'

Mrs. Dare went on her way, her bright face grave with musing, as we all must do at times, on the problem of human misery— of the untowardness of fate to those flung to its mercy.

'Poor things!' she said at last—'*poor dear* things!' and looked up to see Jack standing against a rock close by.

His face was pale, but there was a ghost of a wan smile playing round his lips at her last observation. Seeing which, Mrs. Dare flushed hotly.

'How good of you to wait for me!' she said hurriedly, driven out of her usual self-possession. 'I did not expect you to remember me.'

'I don't think I ever forget you,' said Jack quietly. 'Forgive me for keeping you waiting so long,' he added presently.

'I wasn't waiting,' replied Mrs. Dare, with a fine disregard of truth—'I was seeing about my washing. I would have waited till morning gladly, *if*——'

' Ah,' said Jack, with a shrinking sound in his voice, ' life is all " ifs " and " buts." '

When they came in sight of the camp, Jack paused.

' You have had a dull walk. I am a dull fellow always, am I not ?' he asked, with an uneasy laugh ; ' and worse than usual to-day. They say Freddy has all the wits of the family.'

' They can say what they *like*,' returned Mrs. Dare, with a gesture of disdain.

' Ah well,' said Jack, ' I have not much to care about—now; but if you will keep a corner in your kindly heart for me, I shall value that—always ; and thank you for your goodness, your patience to-day. Do you know what I heard a man say once was your greatest charm ?' he asked suddenly. ' We all know you are good to look at,' with a smile.

' Don't flatter—but tell me.'

' I am no hand at that,' returned Jack. ' He said you were sympathetic.'

'Am I?' said Mrs. Dare, smiling.   'I had never thought so.'

'Yes, it is right enough.   You are always in tune with one's feelings, one's moods— everyone's, I mean——'

'Ah, that arises from instinct, probably —a much lower thing.   I share it with the animals, you see.'

'A darned pity for the world the animals should have *that* monopoly,' remarked Jack, following her with his eyes as she left him.

CHAPTER IX.

LOVE TO HONOUR'S CALL MUST YIELD.

ULIA, you would make a first-rate poor man's wife! You are uncommonly handy;' and Robin laughed as they sat together, some hours later, packing a basket of crockery ready for the start homewards.

'It is not a thing I ever intended to be,' replied Miss Wynyard scornfully.

'Supposing you had fallen in love with such an individual?'

'I should have had to fall out again—quickly. Papa is the last man to tolerate such a thing. We are poor, you know,' she said half proudly, half shrinkingly.

' " My face is my fortune, sir," ' returned Robin gallantly.

' Just papa's view. He says no woman need mind being born poor if she is sufficiently handsome.'

' No, her possibilities are limitless. It is only a question of opportunities then.'

' Opportunities in South Africa are *not* limitless.'

' Is that why you have so misused yours ?' asked Robin, laughing.

' Have I ?' returned Miss Wynyard, with a smile. ' Do you want me to enumerate your advantages?   I fancy you must know them.'

' When I look in my bankers' book ?' asked Robin mischievously.

' When you look in your looking-glass,' responded Miss Wynyard, in the same tone.

' Thanks, fair lady. I wonder what Mr. Wynyard would have said if I had arrived with my looking-glass in my hands to ask his favour ?'

' Oh, papa——'

. ' Yes. I suppose he would have been unpleasantly personal, naturally—a little rude.'

' Not rude—you are such a gentleman, Robin——'

' But he would have shown me the door.'

' Yes. But I do not suppose you would ever have come in at it then.'

' No,' reflected Robin ; ' to enter upon poverty with a woman, you require some compensation.' Aloud, he said, ' I should not have ventured.'

His betrothed glanced at him under her eyelids as she handed him the last teacup. He had been chained to her side this day, and she was gratified by her success. She had adorned her beauty with much care, for she was aware that in that lay her chance to enslave him. A nobler woman might disdain such an offering, but Miss Wynyard had been educated to practicalities, and knew her own requirements. A salve to her pride that the world—which would not inquire into its validity—should see him burn incense at her shrine ; a hold over him to grease the wheels of life in days to come, which might require tolerably extensive lubrication—*voilà tout!* His heart was beyond her reach! Well, hearts are at ¡a discount in Babylon !

Miss Wynyard smiled on Robin, as they chattered on, as sweetly as if her heart really spoke through her eyes—and mused inwardly as she did so. We may aspire to rule the world, our sovereignty may be widespread, and yet one simple insignificant life may remain ever beyond our compass. Miss Wynyard knew such problems were, but she would not let them vex her. She would cast her bread upon the waters with all her skill. It was not impossible it might return to her after many days.

'We have had a pleasant day,' said Robin, as he closed the basket with a slight sigh.

'Yes,' she replied gently, as she leaned towards him ; 'and to-morrow I am going. I—am—sorry.'

He looked at her. A soft sigh swelled her bosom and gave point to the words ; her dark eyes seemed to hold his own with their unfathomable glance, while a mournful smile played round her lips—in the dusky light how exquisite was that face!

A blood-red moon rose swiftly above the horizon into the clear sky, and shed its rays over them—that mystic spell of moonlight! Under it her bewildering beauty seemed to touch and quicken on his senses, as deft fingers press the notes until they swell into a full harmonious chord of music. He had looked long silent—now he spoke eagerly :

'My queen, the time will soon come to us when you will *never* go!'

A flash of triumph blazed in her eyes, which she turned aside to hide, as he kissed the hand he had raised to his lips—

passionately. But a thought struck across his heart, cold and dulling, even in that moment, and he muttered as he left her side: ' My birthright for a mess of pottage!'

Seymour was resting upon the mossy bank where the feast had been held. Mrs. Dare had been sitting there for an hour, and he had been lying at her feet talking to her.

The moon rose for them, too, and he sat up and looked at it.

' What a beautiful scene!' said Mrs. Dare thoughtfully.

' Simply perfect,' replied Seymour, in a dreamy tone.

The intoxicating sense of happiness, of something more full and vivid than happiness—of joy—was stealing over him. It seemed to him that that ecstasy of content must be joy, that unshadowed thing that lays its own wondrous glory on a life once and again, no more—on some never, till they reach where it lies beyond the shadows.

He looked over the vast glittering stretch
of country.

'Glorious !' he muttered to himself. 'Who
can say there is no heaven upon this
earth ?'

Even as he spoke she got up and moved
away.

'I must make a little bouquet,' she said.
'I always keep a few flowers from any
place where I have spent a very happy
time, and then I label them. Horribly un-
romantic, isn't it ? But if I did not, I
might not remember.'

She flitted here and there gathering
buds and blossoms, and he watched her,
wondering what it was about the lines of
this woman's figure, about her very walk,
that so realized his idea of perfect and
unique beauty.

'I should know her among a million,'
he thought, 'and I suppose when a woman
once touches a fellow like that, it is all up
with him. I might have known it all long

ago, only it seems one's destiny to be blind and a fool here. How she struck me that first day as unlike others, and I listened to every word she spoke, though she did not notice me! So clever, so lovely and gentle, how can one *help* falling in love with such women? and yet it is death to your peace if you cannot win them, because they dwarf all others into shadows for ever. It·is not her beauty I care for either, it is *herself;* for I would marry her when she was sixty, if I could, and be prouder of her then than— Ah, God, what shall I do when it is all over?'

'What are you dreaming of?' she said. 'Twice have I asked you, O ungallant cavalier, to hold down that branch.'

He rose in silence; his head was going, he knew it; his heart was beating madly. That last hour spent alone with her had been too happy, too sweet, after the companionship of the last few days. His idolatry had grown apace.

And now it was as if they were in the great moonlit world alone.

But he held the branch down, and tried to fight his battle. One of those hard battles over self, to fight which we are told is the purpose for which we are put here, and verily it seemeth so.

Her white shapely fingers, with their sparkling jewels, flashed about among the flowers as she secured her treasures ; then, in their wanderings, he suddenly felt their warm touch.

He let the branch go with a sharp crack ; it sprang far above them as he threw up his head.

'Give me some of those flowers,' he said hoarsely, ' that I, too, may *remember.*' His eyes met hers at last.

She gazed at him, and the beautiful brown eyes dilated ; the flowers dropped slowly from her fingers.

'Ah! you know at last—yes—I have betrayed my secret!' he said wildly, throwing himself on his knees, and pressing those hands to his lips again and again.

'Yes; don't speak—I know what you would say—this must be the end of it. Yes, I know—it would have come in a few days—it must come *now.* Well, I am sorry—no, I am glad—I shall not go away, and you never know how I have cared. But I would have spared *you,* if I could ; I have wanted to go without this, but it has come so. I have tried, indeed, for I am not worthy a thought of yours, much less a sorrowful one. Never mind, you will forget; but *I*—oh, my love—my love—I cannot look my life in the face!'

He was holding her hand pressed tightly across his face, and he was shaken as with a passing storm where he knelt.

'Heavens ! that you should *dare*——' The words came slowly from her trembling lips. She had turned a ghastly white.

'*Don't,*' he said pitifully, 'don't!' Then he took her hands firmly in his and rose

from his knees. ' Listen l' he said gravely.
' The feeling I bear you. is too pure and
reverential to do you harm—if you were an
angel from heaven it could not sully you—
and I shall. be a better man my life through
for having known and loved you. I have
never dared to love you otherwise, knowing
how hopeless it was ; but I *could* love you,
I think, as never man loved woman before,
and I would cut off my right hand to shield
you from sorrow. You are dearer to me
than aught on earth ; but so—you shall not
suffer for me—the fault is mine and the
punishment. I will say good-bye to you
now. Will you be content then—will you
forgive ?'

' Content! Can I be *content* that such a
thing has come to you——'

She was not a woman to mistake dross for
gold, nor yet one to rejoice that her own
being should have had the power to thus
score a life in its opening years. She knew
the quality of this love now—the metal of

the man who had given it. Her heart was
securely anchored. She was only shaken,
as we are by the passing breath of another's
grief and anguish. What did it mean for
him? A life's darkness, perhaps.

'Will you'—he said unsteadily—'will
you give me one of those flowers in token
that you will try to forget my madness of
to-night, and, when it is gone, that *then* you
will think of me as a—friend ?'

She drew one out, and gave it to
him.

' You have thought a great deal too highly
of me,' she said, in the sweet voice that
trembled despite her utmost efforts. ' You
will know it when your time comes, and
will recognise that this was only a momentary folly.'

'I shall keep it while I live,' was the
steady response, 'in memory of the first
woman who has touched my heart, and, as
I believe—before God—the last !'

' *Hush !* ' she said imploringly, moving

away. The pathos of the words moved her
to pain.

. He threw himself down on the bank, as
the last gleam of her white dress disappeared
amongst the bushes below, and looked again
over the beautiful moonlit country. The
same, yet not the same to him. A strip of
African veldt, with the magic faded off it.

* * * * * *

He came to her side as the cries of the
drivers gathering in the bullocks resounded
on all sides, and the saddle-horses were
led in.

'I was to drive you home,' he said.
'Jack asked me, because Helmsley is going
to take Mrs. Craig in his cart, as she was so
shaken by the waggon; and Jack said he
felt inclined to ride the "Devil," which is
Helmsley's horse, and no one else can.'
Some instinct told Mrs. Dare that Jack
would rather be alone with his own sad
thoughts. 'It would look odd if we altered
it now, and——'

What he wished or thought, he did not add.

Mrs. Dare looked up at him with a shade of perplexity on her face.

' *You may trust me.*   I will transgress no more written or unwritten laws.'

' That is sufficient.   I will come.'

Presently Jack joined them.

' Look here,' he said; ' you must take the other road, Seymour.   I have told the waggon-party so.   We need not try that Blue river again.'

' *Bless you !*' said Mrs. Dare emphatically.

' And you had better look out !' continued Jack over his shoulder, as he rode off. ' Moonlight has a loose shoe, and Starlight will jib like one o'clock if the shadows are not to his liking.   But lick him up! There is no vice in them—only a bit cranky. They *will* tumble down, both of 'em, if they can ; but that's of no consequence.   Their knees are fairly smashed now.'

' Anything else ?' yelled Seymour.

'No, nothing. Yes—stay! I dropped the whip this morning. If you should see it, pick it up, will you? And come home safely. Good luck!'

'Good luck!' roared Seymour. 'If you have got any more of that sort of luck, you can take it with you!'

Mrs. Dare was wrapped up in shawls and rugs in the spider till, as she said, 'I feel like a mummy ought to feel.'

'We will follow in Helmsley's wake,' said Seymour.

And then they started on their lonely journey, those two whose lives had thus touched.

It was not an eventful one. They talked on indifferent subjects, or sat in that sympathy of silence which has a greater charm than words for natures that are at all akin. Only once did Lucas Seymour touch on personal matters, when he said that a week ago he had heard from an uncle who had lately come into his property, and was

33—2

childless, proposing to adopt him as his heir.

'It is nothing wonderful,' he added, 'but well-to-doism for a fellow like me. I did think of refusing it, though I suppose he would have thought me mad to prefer being an ostrich farmer; but now I am going to him.'

Except for the grave tenderness that seemed to mingle involuntarily with each trifling service he performed for her, Mrs. Dare might well have fancied that that moonlit scene of love and despair had been but a nightmare of her imagination. He drove quickly, though he felt as if he must cry 'Hold!' to those flying minutes full of the pathetic charm that the shadow of worse days to come can confer on them.

Afar off through the still night came the thunder and grumble of the waggon, the shrill cries of the Kafir drivers, and the resonant crackling whirr of their whips; in front was silence, with the far-reaching

stretches of veldt sparkling like silver, and
only the distant moving shadow of the cart
they were following. Why could they not
go on thus for ever, with the quiet, lazy jog-
trot of the animals to draw them on over
the silent land, with that beautiful face to
smile through life by his side? Only a
dream, truly; but is not love ever a dream?
What is all life but a great dream—eternity
a greater? Who can say more of a dream
than that he knows not whence it comes nor
whither it goeth?

'I am tired, and so thirsty!' remarked
Mrs. Dare, when many miles had rolled
away behind them.

'Are you?'.replied Seymour. 'We shall
pass Bordingley's. I will stop there, and
see if I can get you a glass of milk. The
first I should like to cure you of, but I am
afraid I cannot.'

CHAPTER X.

SLEEPY HOLLOW.

HE night-wind was cold, and Mrs. Dare shivered in her wrappings, and cast anxious looks at the high bush that now closed them in on each side.

'Here we are! This is Bordingley's!' said Seymour, as they rattled round a sudden bend.

'What a funny little place!'

'Yes, and he is there—I see by his fire.'

'Is his fire out of doors, then?'

'Most everything is out of doors at Bordingley's,' returned Seymour, with a smile. 'Bordingley! Hi! Hi!'

'Who the devil are you?' shouted back a voice.

'Hi! Here!'

'If you think I am curious about you, you are out of it. And I'm busy!' yelled the voice again.

'Hi! Come down here, you lazy beggar!'

After a few minutes' delay a young man appeared in a bright-striped shirt and dark trousers, making his way down a path through the bush.

'Ah, it's you, is it? Where you stowed your legs to-night?' he inquired.

'How do?' returned Seymour, as he came through the little gate that cut off his domain from the road. 'Here's a lady— but very likely you know Mrs. Dare—tired and thirsty. I thought perhaps you would give her a glass of milk.'

'I beg Mrs. Dare's pardon, and I am most happy to meet her at last,' he replied pleasantly, turning to her. 'You are indeed welcome to anything my cabin affords, but that, I regret to say, is not milk. Cows did not come in to-night,' added Mr. Bordingley reflectively.

'Just remembered it?' inquired Seymour.

'Yes, this very minute. Wonder where the brutes can be?' said Mr. Bordingley, casting a bewildered eye over the moonlit landscape.

'Don't go to look for them now, please,' entreated Seymour.

'No, no; to be sure. Still, I'd take kindly to knowing where they are,' mused Mr. Bordingley.

'And you have none of their contents by you?'

'I have a little cream. *Bet* you those cattle are in the pound, Seymour!' cried Mr. Bordingley suddenly, with an air of relief. 'That beast Muller has put in a crop of barley within a stone's-throw of my kraal, and they are usually going in faster than I can fetch 'em out. That's it! He has pounded them twice this week already.

I'm glad that struck me. It worries me
not to know *where* the cows are, of a night.'

' I'm sure I am glad you are pleased.'

Mrs. Dare laughed.

' Ah, yes,' said Mr. Bordingley, with a
faint smile. ' Time was when *I* hadn't
learnt to take the insides out of grief like
that, and call it pleasure. I suppose they
have not got the trick in England yet, but
in a country like this it comes to you quite
naturally in time. When a man tells you
he has had a "joy" here, you know he
means that he has got a weight off his
mind, which will leave him room to worry
over something else. Now, Mrs. Dare,
would a cup of tea do for you instead?
That was what I was going to offer you,
when the pound strayed into my head.'

' Thank you ; it sounds delicious,' replied
Mrs. Dare. ' And I am so cold.'

' Will you not get out, and walk into my
kitchen?—there is a fine fire there. It
sounds rather like " Will you walk into my

parlour?" But I assure you I have no webs except stumps; no roof, alas! but the sky.'

'I fall a prey to curiosity, like the fly. I should like to see your kitchen, and above all, your fire.'

'Why didn't you come to the picnic?' inquired Seymour, as he handed Mrs. Dare down.

'My dear fellow, if you had to cook for yourself from January till December, you would not see the fun of taking a holiday to do a little extra! Of course, that is only my chaff. Now, *why* was it?' Mr. Bordingley tapped his forehead sharply once or twice. 'Ah, yes, I remember—it came so. I have one boy, you know—*some* good points—but he is a "vagrant." Sometimes he turns up, sometimes he don't turn up— not his fault—just as the fit takes him. Well, he knew yesterday that that horse was away over the Grass Hoek—twenty miles good—and he knew that *he* should fetch him, not I, so he *didn't* turn up!

Quite simple—when you come to look at it square. There is nothing complicated about this great country ; you can bet all your guineas on the way things will go, and double your capital every day—if you can get the uninitiated to take it up! Now, Mrs. Dare,' as he handed her in at the gate, ' welcome to Sleepy Hollow!'

' Is that what you call it?' she asked, laughing.

' Yes ; what's in a name? but that is a heavy comfort to me at night. What between cows (not mine, as you may see) rubbing themselves against my bedroom window in mistake for a post, rats running about the larder with my traps at their tails, bucks breaking through the fences after the cabbages, and tigers catching their supper in the " kloofs," I don't see much of the thing but its title.' Mrs. Dare followed her conductor up the path, while he continued cheerily : ' Yes, it's true ; I feel like going mad with yearning after sleep some-

times, till I say those words over to myself
and get soothed. No man *does* in Africa
until he becomes a prey to his imagination.
That is my house, and I will rechristen it
in honour of your visit if you can make a
suggestion.'

' Oh, I could not *improve* on your idea,'
said Mrs. Dare, as gravely as she might.

She looked round her with curiosity.
She saw a small house built of smooth
timber, roofed with shingles, and apparently
containing three rooms ; a flower-bed near
it in bright bloom ; at a little distance a
Kafir hut. At right angles to the house,
well away from it, a large block of bush
cleared in the centre in a circular form,
with long branches meeting overhead, and
woven together with reeds to form a square
of thatch. In the middle a roaring log-fire
with posts and crossbar over it, from which
swung a kettle, and camp pots and saucepans stood alongside. A log-bench and a
rustic chair were on one side of the fire.

Mrs. Dare held her hands out over the blaze.

' What a nice little arrangement, when it does not blow or rain !' she said. ' But why don't you cut down the rest of the bush ? it must be a little eerie when the fire is low.'

'For the very reasons you have mentioned, sun, rain, and wind—it is a shelter from all. I am going to cultivate the decencies some day, and put up an iron kitchen—at present this works. Plague that pot ! it always boils over my toes.'

' Don't you let your boys cook ?'

' Generally, when they first come ; but in the end I find I can suit myself best.'

' Where are your lands ?' inquired Mrs. Dare.

Mr. Bordingley pointed away through an opening in the bush. Mrs. Dare, looking out, saw highly-cultivated lands wide in extent, with heavy crops on them, beautifully laid out.

' That is something to be proud of!' she exclaimed.

' I have not much else to be proud of,' said ·Mr. Bordingley, with the ghost of a sigh.

' What do you do in the evenings ?' asked Mrs. Dare sympathetically ; 'isn't it lonely then ?'

' I don't do much in the evenings,' answered Mr. Bordingley thoughtfully. ' If the animals happen to be in, I sit over this fire and smoke ; or if it turns cold, I go inside. Then I attend to the rats. I take the opportunity, for I have not much leisure sometimes for nights together.'

' The rats ?' queried Mrs. Dare.

' Yes ; the old knowing hands sheer clear of traps, you know. So I sit down quiet against the wall with a candle that I shade with my hand, and a big stick ; and so I lay up for them, and I generally land two or three. It takes hours of watching quiet sometimes, till I feel all over like a cat ;

but what of that? there is nothing else to do, and that's useful, anyway.'

'Dear me! and you have never tried a cat?'

'Yes, I had a cat once; but the cats here are different, somehow, to the home cats. They don't *look* as if there would be anything wrong with them, any more than other things do; but they dawn on you in time. That one of mine had been white, but she'd lost her colour, and people used to be always asking me when I should find time to wash the cat; and I didn't like *that*. Then she *would* lick out the saucepans, and sleep in them after she had done; and as I *knew* it, I didn't feel comfortable. Besides, she didn't fancy mice—colony cats don't— so I thought we should like one another better at a distance, and I gave her away to a friend.'

Mrs. Dare sat on the bench and mused over her host's confidences, whilst he whistled away cheerily over the teapot.

She could not help thinking of his simple, honest, courageous life, and studying him with friendly interest. The firelight glancing on his face showed her the puckers and lines of worry on his forehead from that long ' pulling against the stream ' he had comically described; and it also showed her, lingering still round the mouth in repose, the half-haughty, half-careless expression which is apt to betray that a man has not sprung from the hewers of wood and drawers of water.

' Blood tells even here ; he will not be beat,' thought Mrs. Dare, smiling at her own slang expression.

Max O'Rell might well say again what has been said before, that John Bull is a born colonist, and all his sons take after him ! When we see young men sprung from good old stock, with fine brains, who have been well educated and coddled and cared for, and in the years of their early manhood turned aside with a shudder from a crumpled rose-leaf, scattered over the world—on lonely sheep-stations in Australia, cattle-ranching in America, farming on the wild plains of the Cape, pioneering their way—through hardships and dangers and loneliness inexpressible—to existence or to fortune, with the pride and the courage which command our respect, we look at them with wonder, and are inclined to say : What a waste of such a life, or such talents, on those solitudes !

Is it ?

They build up their *country's greatness ;* in individual instances their own, by dragging fame and fortune out of the very teeth, as it were, of opposing influences. Perhaps they fail to accomplish the second, since only a limited number may reach those front ranks ; or prematurely they fall a prey to the climate or the hardships ; or the heart-sickness which they have fought off lays hold of them, and saps their life, and they slip out of the harness quietly

and cheerfully, and with the same calm
fortitude with which they have worn it. .
It might have succeeded? but it didn't.
Well, every man must take his chance, and
the fault was not theirs. So their comrades
lay them in their quickly-made graves, and
shed a tear over them, and go away and
forget, for life and its struggles are yet
before them; but the traveller muses by
that neglected grave in the wild station,
and asks, for what *object* has he lived and
toiled, and suffered and died?

The young soldier who forms a billet
for a bullet, and sleeps in *his* uncared-for
grave on many a battlefield, we say died
gloriously. doing his duty, and we cast
aside regrets and reproaches over his
grave—he has served his purpose. What
we say of one we may say of the other :
he lived his life like a hero, and he died
doing his duty—we may swear it! And a
grateful country will remember one as
much as the other!

But what matter to them? They have both served the Great Purpose; both died in harness, and both gone to *rest*. For, whatever their creed, no one who has looked on a dead face can doubt *so far*.

Mrs. Dare was roused from her musings over the blaze by her host presenting her with a cup of tea. She took it with a smile of thanks.

'I am enjoying myself immensely,' she said. 'It is like a bit of life out of a book.'

'Would you rather live it, or write it?'

'I might write it, possibly; I could not live it. It must require great force of character to live like this, so lonely, so self-dependent. Why don't you marry?' added Mrs. Dare suddenly, as her eyes lighted upon the teapot with its suggestive train of ideas.

'Marry!' ejaculated Mr. Bordingley, opening wide his eyes. 'Who should I marry? A Kafir? The only woman who would suit this life would be one with a

34—2

precious strong body and no mind, and she
would not suit *me,* even if I could leave
her on the farm with the other fixin's when
I made tracks. I am engaged to a girl at
home,' went on Mr. Bordingley thoughtfully; ' but I suppose she will get tired of
it some day, and take up with some other
fellow. I try to write to her sometimes,
to tell her I think about her. I haven't
time to do it, but I would do it if I could,
so it don't matter telling her. But just as
I have got the pen within range of the ink,
something turns up. I have sat on my
doorstep sometimes for hours, doing fads,
and watched the sun fade off those hills,
and the moon come out and creep up and
up, till I have felt dazed with the lack of
sound to break the stillness, and I have got
so reduced that I'd have *welcomed* old Muller
after the pound-money. But no, I can go
on feeling like that till I am tired of it,
and start feeling some other way. But
take out my writing-case, and things don't

come—they crowd. Boy's head round the
door stuttering to bring out half a dozen
catastrophes at once, not knowing which
deserves first place : Dutchmen for liquor ;
cow in the garden ; pig in the fireplace—
anything you can dream of that will batch
a letter, and the mail goes without. If I
married, I expect I should be glad when
my wife got in the pound along with the
cows—to know the end of her misfortunes
for that day at least. And when she
died, which I guess she would do, after
a bit, I suppose I should lay her in her
grave with much the same feeling, poor
soul! No, Mrs. Dare, I am young and
strong, and I can climb, and I shall, if I
live; but I would rather not look on at a
wife climbing, even,' added Mr. Bordingley
cheerfully, 'if I had time for such things,
which, 'pon my life, I haven't!'

Mrs. Dare agreed that marriage did not
promise; and then, having finished a really
delicious cup of tea, they started down the

path together, and while Seymour drank his, she wrapped herself up in the spider, and pressed a warm invitation on her host to come and spend a long day and sleep on the following Sunday, which, as he remarked, was the only day on which he had time to remember whether he was alive or not.

' I believe I shall die some day without noticing it, when I am awful busy,' concluded Mr. Bordingley, ' and go on just the same, hopping all over the place like a parched pea, until the Sunday comes, or the next chap wanting to bury me.'

' Bye-bye!' said Seymour, as he shook hands, and gave an admonitory shake to the reins at the same time. ' It is a long one, too.'

' Where are you off to, then ?'

' England.'

' Phew! I'm awful sorry. See you back some day. You couldn't stand England after this place. 'Tisn't likely.'

' Look me up when you come home, will

you? I will send you out that pistol you want before the year's out ; and don't go on living here, old fellow, till you turn into a cow or a cabbage.'

And then they were out of hearing, leaving Mr. Bordingley standing, a lonely figure, at his gate.

' Men like that are the backbone of a colony,' remarked Seymour. ' Turn their hands to everything about a farm. They *must* drive ahead afterwards, because they bring practical knowledge to everything they undertake.'

' I admire him immensely,' replied Mrs. Dare ; ' and, oh! he is so droll. I do *hope* he won't forget Sunday.'

It was nine o'clock when they drew up to the end of the veranda at Craigmount.

' Hallo !' exclaimed Freddy, rushing out. 'Began to think you were drowned, or eloped, or something !'

Mrs. Dare waited, leaning against the passion-flower-wreathed pillar, while Seymour collected her wraps ; then he brought them to her. Inside they were all talking and laughing round the supper-table.

'I am not coming in now,' he said. 'I am going for a little walk ; so—good-bye.'

She put her hand in his, which he held in a lingering pressure, while he took a last look at the fair face on which the moon shone.

' Say something kind to me, if you can,' he said, with longing earnestness. ' Something that I may remember when life—gets a bit hard.'

' What can I say ?' she murmured, while her eyes slowly filled with tears ; ' Dieu te garde—*toujours.*'

He took both her hands in his and bent over them in silence. Was it to breathe a blessing for her ? She fancied so, but he did not speak. Only he grew very pale, and then he gently dropped her hands. Their eyes met : the saddest farewells in this world are so taken.

*   *   *   *   *

'I say,' said Freddy to Robin, as they sat in the dining-room—eleven o'clock was striking, and Seymour had just passed through with his bedroom-candle in his hand, wishing them a quiet 'Good-night' —'I say, old Seymour's come his cropper! Did you ever see a man look so knocked over? Perhaps next time he starts getting up to enjoy himself, he will remember me, and stop in bed!'

CHAPTER XI.

'COMING EVENTS CAST THEIR SHADOWS
BEFORE.'

'EARD the news?' asked Freddy, as Robin sauntered out to him on the veranda next morning.

'I expect so,' replied Robin. 'When Seymour came in with my coffee this morning, and said he was catching the next Currie boat home, I was somewhat taken aback. Shocks before your eyes are open are always more shocking.'

'I was out here just after sunrise,' remarked Freddy, 'when out he came. He gave me a start; but I thought he looked so melancholy I would try to cheer him up a bit. So I said, “ Hallo ! have not you had enough of it yet ? This is the second morning you have arisen with the sun to enjoy yourself. Take my advice—don't go and do it a third time.”

‘ He smiled a bit wistfully. Then he stuck out his paw, and said, “ Good-bye, Freddy ; I am sorry to say it, for we have been good friends, I think.”

‘ “ Where the devil are you going to ?” I said, jumping out of my chair in amazement.

‘ “ England,” he answered, as coolly as if he had said, Sleepy Hollow over there.

‘ I don't know what I said—something jolly, I hope ; but a beastly thing always sticks in your throat when you want it to come out. However, he did not give me time to say much. He was down over the steps, it seemed, in a twinkling. Jack says he told him all about it, and that he had a good offer at home; that may be, but he didn't like leaving us all when it came to it

—I could see it. I saw him pick a passion-flower off that pole we all lean against and smoke in the evening, and put it in his coat. Oh, I know he was sorry to go—deuced sorry ! He made straight away for his old Kafir hag's hut—the one he has given tobacco to most days since she was paralyzed —and I never threw a good word after him, as I should have done to a dog I liked. I watched him come out and stalk away over the veldt, looking so long and lonely and grey, it gave me quite a turn. People are *so* selfish !' added Freddy fiercely, with a slight tremor in his voice.

Robin leaned over the trellis, and looked away across the veldt with a half-smile on his lips.

'I dare say he was sorry to go ; and, much as we have abused him, I don't suppose there is one of us not sorry to lose him. But don't worry about him, Freddy. Do you remember my saying to you we should be proud of him yet ? And you have

heard of Scotch second-sight? We have not
heard the last of old Seymour, depend on
it. He will come to the front some day, as
sure as eggs is eggs.’

‘ Poor old chappie, I hope he may,’ said
Freddy dolefully. ‘ But I don’t suppose *I*
shall ever set eyes on him again !’

Robin stood alone, when Freddy had
trailed himself drearily down to the lands.

‘ We shall all be scattered soon—perhaps
never to meet again,’ he mused. ‘ It is odd
how people get interested in one another in
a house like this. Ah, well, we were a
pleasant party when I first lay under those
vines, and Seymour slumbered his golden
hours away—it seems a long while ago now
—but we have all had our troubles since
then. I am used to the shadows ; but I
should like to have seen light break for
some of the others before I went on my
way. Poor old Seymour! I hope it is not
too deep. A man’s fancy for an unattain-
able woman older than himself, who will

keep him the right side of the post, has often made a life, not marred it. I wonder what she thinks, if she knows? She has a good heart. Ah, what a crooked, tangled world it is! and what is the purpose of any of it? By Jove, there is Paulett!'—as a single horseman galloped on to the sweep leading to the house. 'Well, the Craigs never have a bedroom empty long.'

Jimmy Paulett swung himself off his horse at the stoop with a cheery 'Good-morning.'

'The top of the morning to you,' returned Robin; 'and, faith, you have earned it! Where do you come from at this hour?'

'The station. I came down by the night train, and borrowed a horse there. I met Mr. Craig in town yesterday, and he told me it was looking fine out here now. So you are here still! I met Seymour as I was coming down—walking, too. I often say my prayers that I was not born an English-man. He told me he was off, and I congratulated him. I said, " Well, you always hated · Africa, and ostriches, and the vile liquor, and all that, so you are in luck's way at last."

' " Well," he said, " it was not my fate to live amongst them, anyway." How fellows abuse our country while they are here, and yet when it comes to leaving I often think they don't half like it, and some have wished themselves back again. He seems to have dropped into a good thing. I will look up Jack.'

' Englishmen *are* cold, it is quite true,' said Miss Wynyard, laying down her novel, as she sat with Mrs. Craig in the dining-room after breakfast.

' What bosh there is in books! Cold— how do you mean ?' asked Freddy inno-cently, from the corner where he was cutting up tobacco-leaves.

' What a silly question ! Why, at mak-ing love and so on—it is well known.'

'Is it?' inquired Freddy, with a diabolical grin. 'I expect *you* never heard one.'

Miss Wynyard's eyes flashed.

'My dear Freddy——' began Mrs. Craig in remonstrance.

'Now *I* have,' continued Freddy tranquilly and pleasantly. 'I was behind a bush one day—I forget how I got there, but there I was, boxed, and I heard it all. Oh lor! it went whizz, whizz, right through me. I don't know how the girl felt, but it took away all my appetite for dinner.'

'Freddy, really——' said Mrs. Craig.

'Here's Mrs. Dare!' cried Freddy triumphantly. 'Let's ask her. Mrs. Dare, please tell us, *are* Englishmen cold? spoons and that, you know. Now seriously, I mean.'

'Who says they are?'

'A beastly book here, and Miss Wynyard; and I and mother say they *ain't.*'

'Freddy *dear*——'

'So you are an odd one—just say, please.'

Mrs. Dare laughed, 'Well,' she said, 'I suppose they are outwardly, but hardly in a *solitude à deux*, I should have thought.'

'You mean they are in public, and not in private. Don't funk.'

'Yes, that is my meaning.'

'Judging from your own experience of course, lady fair,' adventured Jack, with a grin from the doorway.

'Oh, *you* are there, are you?' muttered Freddy.

'How can anyone's individual experience decide such a question?' replied Mrs. Dare, with a smile. 'But I have heard a good many love-tales.'

'And they were *not* cold—just what *I* said, Miss Wynyard. Now was that before or after you met Dare?' inquired Freddy modestly. 'Oh, *please don't* blush; it makes me feel all over the shop.'

'Ah, Freddy, you are the plague of my life! Of course I meant other people's.'

'Well, I *am* surprised!' said Freddy, with his head on one side. 'Now if *I* was a pretty woman, I should never be taken up with other people's love-stories. I should not have *time*. But then some women know how to enjoy their little selves in this world, and some *don't.*'

'Upon my word, Freddy, I will box your ears!' exclaimed Mrs. Craig with unusual vigour, as he fled from the room.

'I have given it to the "image,"' said Freddy, as he frisked on to the veranda, and made a long nose to Jack; 'said I would! I had made up my mind to be square with her before she left this house, or *die.*'

It was Freddy's last tilt with the foe, for by midday the party had broken up. Robin was driving Miss Wynyard to the station, and even she looked a little romantically back at the house where they had first seemed to know more of each other than society teaches. And Mrs. Dare had taken

an affectionate leave of them all, and was
riding, with Freddy in attendance, to see
some new plantations by the river, and thus
make her way home. Jimmy Paulett settled
himself to a siesta; and Jack?—Jack went
down to the lands, and tried to do spells of
hard work, not caring much what it might
be, only striving to stifle the dull pain that
tugged at his heartstrings whenever he was
alone or unoccupied. In the evening the
weather settled down close and hot, and
during the night a terrific thunderstorm
came on. The forked lightning darted incessantly across the inky clouds, blinding
everyone who did not hide their heads
under their sheets; and the thunder burst
forth overhead in what seemed like one
continuous crashing peal, till the storm
rolled away across the hills, as if to gather
fresh force, and a frightful stillness ensued
that was more awe-inspiring than the
clamour had been. Then, with a faint
muffled peal to herald its advance, it came

working round again, and broke upon them
with a fresh access of fury, to deafen and
terrify everyone with its crackling artillery,
and torrents of driving rain that fell it
seemed in solid sheets, as may have done
the floods of old. So it was a generally
weary-looking party that gathered round
the bright breakfast-table, where the sun
was shining as gaily as if the past few hours
of that terrible night, that had driven sleep
from their pillows, had been a nightmare of
their fancy.

'Something must be done to my room,'
said Jack disgustedly. 'That iron roof is
just like a sieve, and the ceiling will rot.
The water did nothing but splash on my
face last night, every time I thought the
row would let me get to sleep. I tried to
light the candle when the lightning was
worst, and it only sputtered and went
out; I know it was the rain getting in
it.'

'My dear, nothing will keep out rain like

that,' replied Mrs. Craig drearily, in a limp voice ; 'but those new rooms are very badly built. I sat in my dressing-gown, and was terrified to death. I thought every moment the house would be struck——'

'Two of Witbooy's calves were struck dead within a couple of hundred yards of the house, so you were not far out.'

'Oh, Jack, how dreadful ! and think, it might have been us ! Do say grace, dear ; I am always begging you to, and really this morning——'

'You can say it, mater. I dare say you said twenty graces for all us black sheep, last night.'

'Indeed I did,' said Mrs. Craig almost tearfully. 'I thought, suppose I never saw my dear boys again——'

'Ah, I'll be bound you did ! Did you think of a suitable epitaph to fix me up with ?—like that they set over that poor chap in England, "Let the Lord take him now if He will have him !"'

'*Jack dear, don't!* After such a storm, you should think so differently——'

' Quite right, little mother. I have no business to be foolin' here. There is work enough and to spare. I shall have to put on every hand on the farm to repair the damage. And then the boss will be swearing around for a month. Fifty pounds out of our pockets if a penny !' said Jack cheerfully, slapping his.

The door flew open, and the Kafir housemaid appeared before them, with her eyes rolling wildly.

' If you please, Baas, Mr. Kruger must speak with you, when you have done breakfast. He say he must leave directly,' she said breathlessly.

' Kruger leave ! Are you mad——'

' It is not me, my Baas. He say he saw a coffin swing over his bed last night in light so blue, so blue as the sky ; and he is frightened to stay.'

' Well, I'm blowed !' exclaimed Freddy.

'Poor man!' murmured Mrs. Craig, in accents of the deepest pity.

'And he didn't see the devil?' inquired Jack, twisting round in his chair.

'De deovel, Baas?'

'Yes, the devil!' roared Jack. 'Tell him from me if he didn't see him, *he's* all right. He will never go hence without seeing the devil—*no fear*. Take that message—d'ye hear? A cursed pack of fools!' growled Jack, as Naatje fled.

'Oh, Jack, I hope it was only fancy!' said Mrs. Craig gravely. 'I never like to hear of such things.'

'Drunk, I suppose,' said Jack philosophically.

'I don't know, dear—I don't know. He is a very sober man, and it must have impressed him to make him *think* of leaving. Now I think of it—and such things coming together make one feel uneasy—*did* you hear how the cocks crowed at twelve o'clock last night?'

'I did!' answered Freddy. 'I should like to have got up and wrung all their necks. Kitty was on my bed, and it started her howling, and she kept it up pretty well till morning.'

'Dear, dear, Jack! I fear *something will happen.*'

'Something *will* happen,' retorted Jack grimly, 'if Kruger talks of leaving me when I have got twenty carpentering jobs waiting for him this very morning.'

'I wonder if he *did* see it?' said Freddy doubtfully. 'Nice thing to see. And he is a sensible fellow——'

'Yes, he has just proved it,' remarked Jack, getting up to take his cap from the peg. 'However, I must explain to him that it was him *the coffin was after, not the house.* So it is of no use his running away.'

Mrs. Craig passed a busy morning, but she had not forgotten her fears; and when Jack came in to dinner, the first question she put to him was :

'How have you got on this morning ?'

Jack was leaning his head on his hand wearily.

'Got on ? Pretty well. There is a sight of damage done to the vines. I believe there is more thunder coming; I feel so heavy and stupid.'

'And what about Kruger ?' asked Mrs. Craig anxiously.

'Kruger ? oh, hang him ! He sticks to his story, and sticks to going. I would not let him leave to-day, and to-night I am going to change his room.'

'He *does* believe it, then ?'

'Believe it ! I should think so. He is all of a tremble, and looks scared out of his wits. Jackass ! to give up a good berth for a pack of old women's nonsense. Two or three of the Kafirs got hold of it, and of course it is spreading about amongst them like wildfire. I wonder how the Dares fared last night ? a Kafir has come in, saying the river is coming down.'

'Sure to, after this,' chorused everyone.

'Not yet though,' said Jack. 'To-morrow, at earliest.'

The afternoon was dark and lowering. At five o'clock Jack was in the meal and corn storehouse watching Klaas filling buckets of corn. He was idly weighing the barley and letting it tip back again into the bin, while the Kafir gossiped to him.

'Take that bucket round to the stables, and then come back. This will be the last, and I want to lock up.'

'Ja, ja, Baas.' And Jack filled the bucket while he was gone, and then stood and waited.

'What is the matter with me? I feel like lead,' he said impatiently, as he let the grain fall slowly through his fingers. 'I think I will go and have a cup of tea with Paulett and Adair—they look jolly enough on the stoop. Bah! you would think *I* had seen a coffin, instead of that fool Kruger!'

Klaas returned, sighing and swinging his buckets. Jack handed the other to him, and took up some barley in the measure.

' Look out !' he said, turning round sharply, as the Kafir knocked the bucket against the door-post. ' You will spill it all. Hallo !'— looking out—' whose waggons are those going down to the river ?'

Across the open sweep of veldt visible from the door two waggons, with snowy-white tents and long teams of oxen, were slowly passing.

The Kafir shaded his eyes with his hand, and looked long.

' I dunno, master,' he said, relapsing into English.

' Why don't you know ?' asked Jack. ' You know every waggon in the valley.'

' That is not a valley-waggon, master,' returned the man at length, sullenly.

' Whose is it, then ?' asked Jack sharply.

The man's manner awoke his suspicions.

What was this something that was coming upon him, nearer and nearer, with stealthy steps ? He longed to lay his hand upon it. Back to his memory came his mother's words, 'I'm afraid something is going to happen, Jack,' and they no longer seemed incongruous or foolish.

'Curse it all !' he muttered. 'Am I going the way of all the rest ? Here, stop !' he said to the Kafir, who was slinking away with his bucket. 'Why the mischief don't you answer my question ? Put that bucket down, and look till you do know.'

'Does the Baas wish me to tell him ?' queried the Kafir, turning a frightened, unwilling face towards him.

'Wish you to tell me ! Didn't I ask you ? Are you in your senses ?'

'Baas must remember I did not want to tell him. Baas must not be cross. Those waggons are Mr. Muller's waggons.'

'Well, what of that ?'

'Oh, nix ' (nothing), said Klaas.

'If you are keeping anything back——'
began Jack threateningly.

'Ah! does not the Baas guess, that he *will*
make me say to him—and he hear it too
soon? That is Mr. Muller's waggon, and he
was married to Missie this morning. Missie
is there now.'

'*You lie*——'

'Nie, my Baas, I not lie. They should
marry in two days, but now the floods will
come, and Mr. Muller he wanted to be at
his farm ; he frightened of the floods for his
sheep. The minister was there, and he
frightened, too, that he should not get back
to town for de Sunday. So he married them
both this morning, and they go to home
now. And they will give their feast at his
farm in one month, and all the Dutch for
miles '—with a wave of his hand—' will go ;
for Baas Muller is rich—rich! That's all,
Baas.'

And Klaas swung up his bucket and
departed.

The barley-grains went on dropping through Jack's fingers slowly — slowly. Where was he? What was he doing? Was it a year ago, or just now, he heard those words? They were dreadful words; for they were burning, burning, beating into his brain now, yet he could not grasp the sense of them. Had they said Dollie was *married—his* Dollie? No, it was not true. He was dreaming. The mother had said something was going to happen; that was not true either. Was he going mad, that such dreams, such terrible thoughts, came into his mind to bewilder him? There was a red mist before his eyes, and, though he passed his hand across, it did not seem to clear. He felt stupid, cold, and, like a man groping his way in the dark, he stumbled out of the storehouse. Ah! there were the waggons; he could see them even through the mist. Did they say *she* was there? Passing *his* house with — with——

He stood gazing at the waggons.

'No, no,' he said, with a sickly smile. *'Mine* to-day ! *Mine* to-day ! Yes, yes, I know, the last days ; but *mine—to-day !'*

'Don't take on, master,' said Klaas's voice in English at his elbow.

'Klaas,' said Jack, speaking in a low, unsteady voice, and grasping the Kafir's arm, 'I—I—am not well, I think. I fancy I have had a shock——'

'Yis, master.'

'Did you say—did anybody say—tell me what you *did* say about—Miss Dollie ?'

'I said she was married to Baas Muller.'

'Is it true ?'

The Kafir pointed rapidly to the sky.

'It is true, master. See ! I take my oath !'

Jack turned away.

'It doesn't matter,' he said feebly.

Klaas looked after him, and shook his head.

'How the English love their women !' he

said. 'They do say Miss Dollie cry—cry all the day, too. Ah! she wanted Baas Jack—so should I if I was a woman.'

Klaas stood looking until he saw Jack turn the corner of the house.

'Goed master! I suppose the Great God up there doesn't like goed masters,' he said in a puzzled tone, as he turned into the stable.

Jack reached his bedroom. The cold air had cleared his senses. Now he knew that he had never really believed this thing would happen. Something would intervene. Well, nothing had intervened, and he was face to face with it now. He stood now on the brink of this great gulf, fixed between his past life and his future one. Should he call upon Death, and descend into the abyss, and know and suffer no more? Or should patient endurance bridge the chasm in time, and he pass over and gather up the shreds of his life as best he might on the other side?

He took out Dollie's picture, that he kept

in an old-fashioned silver case, from the drawer where he had reverently placed it that morning among his little collection of sacred treasures and mementos. It was his custom to look at it after breakfast before he went to his work, and then put it away for the day. He opened it, and, as he did so, the strong man shook like a leaf.

There was that pictured face with its bright smile, taken in the days of her innocence and joy, that he had glanced at so fondly that very morning. How did it look *now?* With a groan, he almost crushed up the case in his powerful fingers ; and, throwing himself on his knees by the bedside, the agony of his soul found vent in words :

'O God ! she was his wife this morning, and I—*never knew it!'*

CHAPTER XII.

DOLLIE'S WEDDING EVE.

'THE last page of that drama folded down,' said Robin to Paulett, indicating the passing waggons, as they sat drinking tea on the veranda.

'I wonder if Jack knows it? Naatje tells me the Kafirs heard it at daylight.'

'Ay, but they beat telegraph wires for transmitting intelligence to each other. Jack, unfortunately for himself, is not a Kafir.'

'Nearly tanned dark enough for one.'

'Lacks the consequence, though. Inflated apes!'

'Poor Jack! I hope he has given up thinking about the girl.'

'Ay, poor Jack!' echoed Robin.

Each looked after the waggons, occupied with his own thoughts.

The heavy clouds were hanging low overhead, and the thunder growling incessantly in the distance. The veldt wore that peculiarly barren, desolate look that African scenery gathers when the sun veils his light, and the range of mountains under that gloomy shadow appeared, with their vast upheavals surmounted by jagged crests, their black yawning fissures, as does our satellite above, a world 'wrecked and torn.'

'Not exactly ideal honeymoon weather,' remarked Robin at last. 'I wish Max Muller joy of that girl. He was determined to have her, in the teeth of everything. I have heard it is not a lucky thing to do,' he added dreamily, looking out to where the lightning was playing with a pale blue glare through a rent in the inky clouds.

36—2

The wind whistled drearily round them, and Paulett shivered.

'Let us go to the smoking-room,' he said. 'It is as cold as June.'

The two waggons with their long teams of fat oxen, followed by the Cape cart in which the wedded couple were to have travelled had the weather been less threatening, passed on their way. In the first was Dollie, seated with her bridegroom at her side ; but though his eyes were turned often on her face, he could read nothing of the thoughts passing in her heart. Through all their lives, probably, that secret chamber of her mind would never be unlocked to him. She had married a husband, but her unwedded soul might long wander through space, seeking wearily its lost half, and refusing to take account of the goods the gods offered for its acceptance.

Dollie had made one stern resolution, to look in the contrary direction when she reached Craigmount ; but, instead of this, it

escaped her to swell the ranks of unfulfilled
intentions, and she found her eyes irre-
sistibly drawn to the place, as it first rose to
view dimly in the distance. She saw the
two figures, later, on the veranda; but her
heart lay dumb, and she knew neither of
them was Jack. She held, she deemed, in
faithful memory every trail of the climbers,
each stone and corner of that house which
had figured so often in her dreams; but it
seemed to be invested by a beauty and a
peace with which her fancy had never clothed
it, now that she was shut out from it for
ever. So will heaven look to the doomed,
we suppose, when they gaze at it through
barred portals.

And she had dreamed once that she might
live there and reign. Yes, reign; for to
Dollie no throne of the earth could have
been half so gorgeous. Ah, no; it was all a
dream; it had always been nothing but a
dream—in her foolish heart she had always
known that. The king was there still, but

he would take another queen some day;
and the kingdom and the sceptre which had
once seemed within her grasp would be
handed to the usurper.

Ah, it was the king himself she craved;
never mind if the palace were in ruins, so
she possessed him for her own. Jack in
rags ! Jack to dwell with her in a Kafir-
hut !

Ah, what bliss is in the dreams of this
world ! What hopes are wrecked with each
passing day, that half fulfilled might have
caused human souls to blossom like the rose !
And yet they rise fairer daily out of their
own cold ashes, lest the tortured heart and
brain should faint and say, ' Methinks this
life is a fatal gift. I will strike to the root
of the mystery. I will know, before my
time, why I came and whither I go.' Craigmount faded from sight, and Dollie felt as
if a cold hand clutched her heart; but it was
only Max's voice speaking to her with a
sneering impatience.

'Ye take interest in that place yet. I mind that house, Dollie, on the morning I went there with my will made up to have you for my wife, or shoot myself. I am not likely to forget it. I have troubled for ye a sore time—but I have won ye at last. Ah, a man can gain a woman, or anything else, if he make up his mind that way. A woman puts the devil into a man sometimes; and when the devil is in you, you have no *fear;* and when you have no fear, there is not a wheel that works that can stop you. That fine Englishman do not trouble himself to come out and wish "geluk" and good-day to the girl he made such a work over. I should think he has forgot you by now, Dollie. These Englishmen are like a "vreug devuur"—so hot and noisy—so soon burnt out. Not that it is any odds to you now— you can laugh at him; for you have a richer man for your husband this day than Jack Craig; and, Almighty! he will not love you worse!'

Max's heavy voice vibrated into silence again as Dollie made no reply, even by a look. But his eyes gleamed uneasily despite the apparent carelessness and contentment of his last words. Did some instinct tell him of the one speck for which those weary eyes of the girl he loved were straining in vain? Did it show him, beyond, that man's powerful frame quivering in agony—for how do the very fibres of the body respond to the mind's anguish—those strong brown hands clutching the bedclothes, as he buried his face in the pillows, in that little chamber that had witnessed many a lonely vigil.

'Baas!' cried a voice — a high, shrill Hottentot voice.

The waggons were nearing the river-bank. A crowd of Kafirs, most of them Jack's boys, stood there. The little Hottentot, September, who still bore the marks of Jack's castigation on his malformed body and a deadly hatred of him in his heart, clambered up into the waggon as it stopped.

' Baas, the Kafirs say the river come down,' he said in Dutch.

Max Muller frowned heavily.

' Foolishness,' he replied, in the same language. ' The storm but the night passed.'

'They say so, Baas.'

' Well, it will not come down before we are across, if it comes the night,' responded Max Muller, with a grim laugh.

' Will Baas speak to the Kafirs? Our leaders are frightened to go on.'

' Blood and thunder! I will give them something to be afraid of.'

And Max swung himself out of the waggon. He approached the group of Kafirs on the bank. There was a dead silence amongst them.

' What is the meaning of this, you set of dunderheaded fools?' he asked fiercely.

' We are not fools,' growled Klaas sullenly. ' It is Baas Muller will be the fool, perhaps, if he does not listen.'

An old man, a strange Kafir with a

tattered sheepskin hung round him, stood out, and said respectfully :

'It is true, Baas—the news bring. We have been looking for the river each minute these three hours.'

'And you may look for it another twelve,' said Max Muller scornfully.

'Well, Baas, it may be. The white men say they can stop a river if they like. It may be, too, they are wise ; but unless Baas is one of those men, he will do well to stop where he is to-night.'

'Stay where I am to-night ! Why, —— it ! I have crossed with the river in sight coming round the bend !' said Max impressively, turning to his own boys.

Gravely the old man answered :

'On a horse, perhaps ; not with waggon —loaded-down waggon, Baas. And the river come slow, and the river come quick ; it will come quick now—the river will be very, very full.'

'Curse it all !' cried Max Muller, in a fury,

as he saw his leaders drinking in the old
man's words. ' Do you think I am mad ?
I want to get to my farm ; I have my wife
in the waggon. When this river comes, it
may be full all a week. Am I to stay on
this bank for that time, because I do not
cross now when I may ?'

' There is a farm there,' said the old man
laconically, and did not see the smile that
ran round among the Kafirs.

But Max Muller did.

' You are drunk !' he exclaimed, with an
ugly sneer, grasping his sjambock.

' Nie, Baas,' was the calm response. ' Baas
may want to get to his farm, Baas may have
all his wives and all his childre in the
waggon, but if Baas is wise he will stop
here. The river may not come before the
waggon is across, but they said it would
come *before the sun set.* But why should I
talk to the Baas ? He knows the danger of
the river as I do—let him go; the white
man is lucky. The Great Spirit help the

white man.' And he sat down on the bank
with his chin resting on his knees.

Max Muller went back to the waggon,
looking angry.

'You hear what the Kafir say—are you
frightened?' he asked of Dollie.

'Oh no!' she replied.

There are times in life when Death looks
inviting. When to lie still in our shrouds,
away from the fret and bustle and the
wondrous jar of life, seems gain to the tortured heart. We cannot fancy the sun will
ever rise again on our lives, and we have not
felt the icy fingers of the destroyer—so to die
is well. And we guard ourselves with less
care than we are prone to do when our souls
are not sick and weary, and look with dull
indifference, at least, on the possibilities of
calamity.

'There is no danger,' said Max.

'Will they not go?' asked Dollie.

'They *must* go, if I am willing. My life
is as precious to me as theirs; and I would

not risk the life of you, my wife, for all I am worth ; but I have not lived here all these years not to know this river by now.'

' It was an unusual storm,' said Dollie thoughtfully.

' These Kafirs love getting up scares, and I cannot wait here even till the sunset, when I suppose these fools would believe. I cannot outspann on Jack Craig's veldt, close to his house, after what has passed between us,' said Max gloomily.

' Oh no!' replied Dollie, with a shiver, thinking of the lover who had loved her so truly. ' Kiss me—kiss me, so that I may dream you are *mine*.' She could almost hear again those words, in which his whole soul had spoken. Ah! it was wicked— they must ring in her ears nevermore. And the girl turned with a faint smile to her husband. ' Let us go on, Max,' she said.

' It shall be so, mijn liefje,' he returned briskly. The near neighbourhood of Craigmount was an abomination to him.

Then came an altercation with his Kafirs. The Boer generally has great influence with the natives, possibly because he makes no pretences, so the native mind is not suspicious of him. The Boer understands him thoroughly, of which he is perfectly aware, and in this case also knowledge is power. Should the native ask, as he is given to do when of an inquiring turn, abstruse questions of an Englishman, he will probably endeavour to take high ground in his answers. If he asked the same of a Boer, the latter would frankly reply that it was God's will, who made one a man and the other a monkey, and the native will accept it unquestioningly; he is by nature a fatalist, and he has great faith in the Boer. The Boer took his country because he wanted it, uses him because he wants him, will treat him ordinarily with perfect indifference, relapsing into something much more disagreeable if he do not do his duty; and, this being understood between them, it is all plain sailing.

The Englishman's reasons for doing as he desires are too complicated to commend themselves to a nature of which the striking keynote is cunning; therefore the Englishman is either a blundering knave with deep designs, or a great fool that takes him for another; and he spends his life playing up, as neatly as he may, to those two English idiosyncrasies. Of fidelity and attachment he is capable in isolated instances, and of the reverence of matter for mind; but until the phrenologist provides him with bumps on the top of his head as well as at the back, he will never bestir himself to understand a problem of which the motive power is supposed to find birth in that admirable bump ' benevolence.'

The Boer, in this instance, was a good master amongst the Dutchmen, and the place was worth holding; so when he accosted the boys, sjambock in hand, with a few determined words, the matter was quickly settled. Only the driver of the second waggon sullenly refused.

'Get down then!' cried Max, in Dutch.

The boy hesitated; but Max's sjambock curling round his shoulders soon settled that dispute.

'Drive that waggon!' he said to the Hottentot sharply.

The Kafir looked discomfited where he stood rubbing his shoulders. He had lost a good berth, and the lesson was not lost on the others, and they began to haul at the oxen and shriek with willing vigour. Max Muller sprang into the first waggon, the Hottentot into the hinder one, and they were moving—rolling swiftly down the sandy banks.

On they groaned, while Dollie looked behind her like Lot's wife, and Max kept his eyes on the oxen. The old man sat on the top of the bank motionless.

'Ai—o—o! softly—softly—smooth!' he said, in his own language.

The leading oxen took the water, and then the yelling and cracking of whips that attends the passage of a waggon across a drift set in.

'The drift is good,' said Max Muller gaily. 'We shall cross quickly, and dry —that old fool!'

'Nacht, nacht!' (night), cried September, cracking his whip as his waggon passed the Kafirs.

As he spoke there was a shrill cry as of a bird away down the river.

Amidst the din the old man's ears caught it. He rose to his feet with a smile and wound his sheepskin round him, but he said nothing. He listened again. Then he spoke one word in Kafir—paused—repeated it louder.

A cry broke from the watching Kafirs as the word reached their ears, which grew into a warning wail. The leader of the second waggon caught it, and stopped his team at the water's edge. September sprang out of the waggon in wild alarm, and joined his cries to theirs.

'Hark!' exclaimed Dollie. 'What is that?' as the cry reached them above the splashing and rumbling and yells of the drivers.

'Nothing,' said Max. 'Only those fools on the bank.'

But he turned his head uneasily as the cry fell, to rise again in a hoarse shout.

'Almighty God, it is the river!' he cried, as a dull roar struck his ears. 'On for your life; there is *time—time!*' he called to his leader in a voice of thunder, as he saw him waver, and knew that ominous sound had reached him too.

The boy dragged madly at the oxen, and Max wielded the whip with the force of desperation, while that warning wail rose wilder from the bank.

The roar deepened. Dollie covered her face with her hands. The Kafir leader gave a yell of mortal terror as he looked up the river, and sped through the stream, that haply he might gain the bank, while the deserted oxen fell back on one another.

Again came that cry from the bank. Too late; no mortal power could save them.

'Curse that Kafir hound!' cried Max, in agony.

They were the last words he spoke, as he flung his arms round Dollie.

With a shriek the girl wrested herself away from that hated embrace. In death she would be *free*. It was her one wild thought as round the bend came that awful wall of rushing water, bearing giant timbers on its bosom.

It is to be hoped in mercy that when human beings are called to face instant death in such guises, when their young pulses are bounding with full health and strength and tenacity of *life*, that their souls are numbed by the suddenness of the peril, and so a lifetime of agony is not compressed into those few waiting seconds.

In an instant it was all over. A dull,

grinding, crushing sound, an upheaval of the water, and the surging torrent swept madly on, bearing a few more fragments on its bosom. The rocks frowned grimly above the scene of destruction, and echoed back a mournful cry : 'Jack ! Jack ! *Good-bye!'*

'Poor Baas Jack!' said Klaas, as the gleam of a blue dress on the brown water caught his eye. 'And all those big, fat bullocks; it is enough to make a Kafir's heart weep.'

The old Kafir smiled an almost happy smile. He was only a half-decayed, stupid old Kafir, and the Dutchman had laughed in the prophet's face—and where was the Dutchman *now?* So! A live ass is better worth than a dead lion all the world over!

CHAPTER XIII.

THE RESCUE.

 CROWD of excited men stood on the river-bank. The wind was blowing at intervals with the force of half a hurricane, and, mingling with the roaring of the water, was so deafening that each one had to shout his loudest to make himself heard at all. The stream was racing past, and had carried down plenty of the flotsam and jetsam of life in the past half-hour. Household utensils, dead cows and pigs, fruits and vegetables, and even a live ostrich, had gone whirling past their eyes ; but they paid but little attention to these, for the great question of a human

being's life or death still hung in the balance
to be determined.

One life at least had been sacrificed.
Across the green slopes where the waggons
had passed an hour before, a few dusky
forms were moving slowly in the light of
the setting sun. They were Kafirs, bearing
between them a rudely-made stretcher on
which lay the bruised and crushed remains
of the luckless man who had received his
sudden call hence just as he had reached
the summit of his ambition, and life, like a
land of Canaan, lay before him.

Max Muller's face was very peaceful, as is
often that of drowned persons, and the
injuries he had received to his limbs were
doubtless caused when the tide first struck
the waggon, before the flood carried him
away. The body had been recovered half
a mile down the river, where it had flooded
low-lying lands in its passage, and deposited
there pieces of driftwood, and this, its
ghastly burden. By the side of the corpse

walked Freddy with his hat off, and the Kafirs toiled on against the wind on their way to Craigmount; for thus, by a strange turn of Fate, must the remains of Max Muller rest in the house of the man from whom in life he would not have accepted a tithe of shelter or consideration.

And Dollie?

Ah, how all the hearts on the river's banks were echoing that question! Had that fair child met with a fearful end, and gone to rejoin her bridegroom in a world where misunderstandings are not, and marriage is not? Her wedding-day had opened in tears and pain—had she gone before its close beyond their reach? or had she yet been spared to the prayers of that frenzied man who stood on the bank, gazing across the water, dulled and stupefied with grief, recking of nothing but the possible answer to the only question of slightest import to him now? He had given her up once that day to man, and the conflict had been beyond measure bitter. Had the very night of all things come now—had he given her up to God? Across the raging waters, as much beyond any aid of his as if she had indeed crossed the dark river, rested the solution of the problem.

About two hundred yards down the river from where the catastrophe occurred, a large tree grew out from the rocks, and some bushes which were now covered by the flood. They caused an eddy there, which had collected driftwood under the branches of the tree, and amongst its small boughs a few feet above the water the watchers on the other side could discern a trail of a woman's hair, a dress that had once been blue. What did that cover? *Dollie?* or some *thing* as inanimate as itself?

There was no means of deciding that question. That she was insensible was evident to all ; she lay face downward across the branch towards the water. Life might have been extinguished in a moment by the crushing force of any of those pieces of timber ; it probably was extinguished by drowning, at least. Such was the conclusion of those on the bank generally, except Jack, who resolutely refused to believe that the spark of life did not still linger. There are some things we dare not believe until they are forced upon us ; 'we feel our very brains reel at their contemplation.

When a Kafir, coming up breathless with the news of the washing ashore of Max Muller's body, had first espied that woman's dress among the branches, Jack, who had just arrived at the spot, looked and acted like a madman. The reaction from the certain despair that had fallen on him—when some one had tried to *break* the appalling news to him, with the usual success of such endeavours—to a gleam of hope, threatened to shake his mind from its balance in presence of the forced inaction.

He had tried to throw himself into the water, in the hope of reaching her—let him perish with her if he could not save her! He only gave way when his friends, employing force first, fell back upon reasoning, and showed him how uselessly he would lose his life, and that, if she *were* alive, he must hold it precious for her sake.

Jack was by no means a noted swimmer, but there was a Kafir among them who was, and who had accomplished wonderful feats sometimes in the way of swimming the river, for trivial rewards. To him Jack turned, telling him to name his reward and go.

But the man shook his head, and said impressively that for nothing the master could offer him would he try to cross the river, running as it was. No man could reach the opposite bank with his life, of that he was positive.

His words carried a sad conviction to the minds of his listeners, of what their eyes had before assured them. Even if a man could resist the force of the current, the driftwood coming down must destroy him.

'If Jacob won't do it, there is no one can,' said Freddy. 'He is a wonderful swimmer, and greedy too; and, of course, Jack would stick at nothing.'

'My dear boy,' Robin had replied solemnly, 'I do not believe it *can* be done by mortal man until the first flush is over.'

'Ah,' Freddy had answered sorrowfully, 'Jack knows the river is rising yet. It *is* hard to think that poor girl may be alive, and we must stay here and watch her die or be carried away.'

Then Freddy had gone on his sad duty, and Jack had paced wildly up and down, turning over mad schemes in his head; and Robin and Paulett watched him in silent sympathy, while the dusk crept over the river and the wind slowly went down with the sun.

When Freddy returned, he whispered to Robin:

'I really tremble for Jack ; it is enough to drive him out of his senses. What a twenty-four hours this has been! The poor mother is beside herself with grief and horror. Somebody has kindly told her that Jack cared for Dollie.'

' Where have you put *him?*' asked Robin.

' In Kruger's deserted room. It was the only empty one away from the house.'

They exchanged glances.

' Yes,' said Freddy, ' it is curious. I never thought of it till after.'

A group of natives had collected on the opposite bank. The Englishmen made offers to them, translated by signs through their coloured brethren. But in vain. Crawl down over a rock on to a rotten frail branch hanging over that water to pick up a dead girl ? Ah, Kafirs might be fools— they were not such fools as that came to !

'O God !' groaned Jack ; 'if *I* were only that side !'

'That branch would not carry your weight for an instant,' answered Robin, 'and she is close to the end of it'—as in truth she was, just resting in a network of small boughs.

'It has risen two inches,' said Freddy, in an awed tone to Robin, looking at the water-mark.

'I dread to look across there each moment for fear she should be gone,' muttered Paulett. 'What shall we do—when it gets dark ?'

'I am convinced we shall have to get Jack away from this,' said Robin gravely, 'or the consequences will be serious.'

Jack was standing brooding by the water with bent head, and hands locked together. Hardly had Robin spoken before he turned round and came quickly up to them.

His head was bare, his hollow eyes gleamed unnaturally ; those few hours of despair had ravaged his face as not ten years of ordinary life would have done.

'Go to the house for a rope, Freddy,' he said. 'I am going into that river. I don't suppose I shall get across, but I shall go mad if I stay here, and I may as well die doing my duty to the girl I love. Do you think I shall ever rest night or day after, if I let her be carried away before my eyes? Get the rope—I have played the coward too long.'

Freddy set his teeth, then he dug his heel into the ground.

'I cannot do it,' he muttered brokenly; 'it is madness. Oh, my brother, do not think of it!'

'Then I must go without,' replied Jack. 'I don't care for the rope for myself,' he said, with a chill laugh; 'but I suppose the mother will want my body.'

A look of shuddering fear swept over Freddy's features. 'He is going mad!' he cried.

Jack was taking off his clothes with eager nervous haste ; he neither looked at them, nor spoke again. But Robin and Paulett walked up to him at once. He swung round like a wild animal at bay.

' *Dare* to touch me !' He said it hoarsely, with deadly meaning, and his eyes gleamed.

' Oh, what can *I* do !' cried poor Freddy wildly. ' What will mother say when I take him back *dead?* Heaven have mercy on us !'

It was almost a shriek, as the boy threw himself between his brother and the river.

' Hark !' exclaimed Robin eagerly. Was Heaven going to answer that forlorn prayer?

Freddy caught at any shred of hope. ' Stop, Jack !—*wait!*' he cried, seizing his brother by the arm. ' This may be some-thing good.'

· They knew what it was now. It was the sound of horses in full gallop ; and as the idea struck them, two horsemen appeared coming down at full speed towards the river.

'It is Dare and his manager!' they all
burst out together.

What a look of joy broke over Jack's
face! Then it faded away again.

'He can do nothing from that side; no
one can,' he groaned.

'Never mind! Wait and see!' cried
Freddy eagerly. 'If ever there was a
fellow full of ideas, it is Dare.'

They saw the riders check their horses
in astonishment; then Dare sprang to the
ground, and gave one glance over the river.
Then he held up a postbag, shook his head
and smiled, as much as to say, 'I am done
after all.'

Presently he put his hands to his mouth
and shouted, they concluded; but no sound
reached them above the roar of the torrent.

'Will those brutes tell him?' muttered
Freddy.

Yes, those brutes would, at their leisure,
for a tall Kafir strolled slowly towards him.

It was an animated colloquy that followed;

the Kafir gesticulating furiously, and Dare rapidly questioning. Then he followed the Kafir down the bank, and looked over.

The others crowded round, adding their version of the affair; but he waved them all away, and stood there alone looking over.

They saw him point to Jacob and ask a question, to which the Kafir replied by a negative shake of the head; then he made a signal to his manager, Clarke, who tied up the horses and came to him, and together they looked over again, and talked earnestly.

'He cannot be thinking of going down himself,' said Freddy slowly.

'He is taking off his coat!' exclaimed Paulett.

'Don't do it—you have a wife!' yelled Jack, with a terrific shout.

What the words cost him everyone guessed.

Dare raised his head, but evidently gained no sense of the words, and went on as before, apparently, in consultation with Clarke.

Presently they moved away from the bank, and the tall Kafir sped away to a hut near, to return shortly with a rope and a reim. Rapidly Dare tested the former, and then fastened it to his belt. He stood one moment on the bank, looking back over the country.

' A thought to "the girl I left behind me," ' muttered Robin. And then Dare waved his hand to them in encouragement, and almost before they had realized he was going, he had begun his perilous descent down the face of the rock. The Kafirs in a line of six, with Clarke at their head, held on to the rope, and it slowly lengthened with his progress.

' If he is used to Alpine climbing he may manage that rock somehow,' said Robin ; 'but what he will do with the rotten timber below is a puzzler.'

' God bless him for a brave, kind friend!'

burst forth Jack, with infinite feeling in his voice.

Down over the rock, hanging on to the mosses and parasites, swaying badly sometimes, then steadying himself cleverly, now with feet, now with hands, Dare passed on in his descent, and at length reached the shelf near which the trunk of the tree grew out horizontally towards the water. The soil and sand slipped with him there, but flinging his arms round the trunk, he raised himself till he could crawl along it to where the branches forked out. Then came a pause, and what seemed to them like an anxious look above.

He carefully tested the next branch below him with his foot, and then slowly let himself down to it, sitting astride upon it.

' Ah, now comes the difficulty,' said Freddy. ' Ten to one the next branch won't bear him, and it is so far ·below. What can he want so much rope for ?'

For Dare had given several sharp pulls

at the rope, and they had paid him out some yards. He swayed violently on the branch, as if to test its strength; then he rose, holding on to it, and held up his hand towards the Kafirs for a whole minute, it seemed. Then they lost sight of him suddenly.

'By Jove! he is in the water!' cried Jack.

'That was a signal to stand hard to the rope, then; it is no accident!' cried Robin reassuringly.

But they looked for him anxiously, only the shadow was so deep on the water they could not discern much. It was a moment of agonizing suspense; then they saw him rise to the surface close to Dollie, and Jack breathed heavily, and the cold beads stood on his forehead. Ah, *he* knew whether it was life or death there!

They saw him fighting with the current, and they had hopes and fears alternately; but he was out of the full sweep of its power. He was bobbing about among the driftwood a long time, it seemed, and then there was a sudden yell from the Kafirs above, and they began to pull in the rope.

Jack staggered back as he saw Dare slowly rising into the tree again. If she was alive, would he have left her there? Or, was he afraid of a breaking-strain for the rope? On, on, until he gained the trunk of the tree, where he again seated himself astride; and they watched him with intense interest as he busied himself with the rope. Then they saw he had something in his hand which he was fastening with great care as to its security to the rope— and then it flashed upon them how it was.

'It is the reim!' cried Freddy. 'He has got it round her, for a sovereign!'

Freddy won his bet almost as soon as uttered, for in another moment they noticed that inanimate figure moving swiftly upwards, and Jack gave a bursting sigh of relief as its distance from the water increased. Dare, from his seat, steadied its progress as much as he could, and stopped it alongside, while he took off his thick woollen shirt and tied it over the girl's head and face. Beyond that they could only trust to the chapter of accidents.

Jack could not watch that upward passage so fraught with danger to her if she was alive, when any moment she might be dashed against the projections on the face of the rock; and he covered his face with his hands, and spent those minutes as we may pray to pass few of our minutes in this life.

A ringing cheer breaking out both sides of the river brought him to his feet with a bound, and he saw that she was on the top of the bank, and that the rope was descending again for Dare, who sat on the tree-trunk waving his handkerchief to join in the general jubilee.

As the rope neared him he made a spring up for it, and caught it with his right hand, while Freddy cried wildly, 'Hooray for

Dare!' but the words were choked off between his teeth, for as Dare seized the rope
and touched the branch again, the rotten
timber swayed under the jerk—cracked—
and fell. A cloud of dust from falling
stones enveloped him as the support left
him, and he swung in mid-air, with only his
right hand grasping the rope. One sicken-
ing sway the rope gave towards the rock, as
it felt his weight, and he threw out his left
arm as if to guard himself.

'Ugh, it's all over!' shuddered Robin, as
Dare struck the rock, but though his head
fell back for an instant, they saw when the
rope swayed out again that he was still
hanging to it.

'He has steel muscles, but he can never
hold on while they draw him up,' gasped
Jack. 'Ah, well done—well done!'

This last exclamation was called forth by
the fact that Clarke had sprung to the edge,
and under his rapid directions the Kafirs
lowered the rope.

It ran swiftly out until the debris of the rock and tree were reached—half in, half out of the water—on which Dare got a slight foothold, while he slipped the loop of the rope under his arms. They noticed that his left arm hung limp by his side.

'Clarke has saved his life. What a mercy he was there!' said Jack solemnly.

'Yes,' returned Robin enthusiastically. 'If those Kafirs had been alone they would have hauled in sharp, and there would have been an end of as gallant a fellow as ever breathed.'.

'That left arm has suffered, I fear,' said Jack, as they saw Dare begin his painful cat-like ascent, using only the right hand for purchase.

How they cheered him all the way up that rock, and what a cheer burst forth when he stood on the top, until the cliffs echoed again ! It went on ringing after he had waved his arm to them, and then fallen on the ground in apparent exhaustion, while the Kafirs danced round him in their excitement.

' 'Pon my soul!' cried Robin, 'they handled that rope well all through.'

'That is one advantage of a Kafir,' responded Jack; 'he will do *exactly* as he is told. But call upon him for ideas—and he is nowhere.'

And then all those figures on the other bank faded from view, and the deep dusk settled down over the scene.

CHAPTER XIV.

IS IT LIFE OR DEATH ?

O *wait !*—it is the hardest thing in this world ; and Jack knew not what signal to look for from Dare.

A quarter of an hour dragged its slow length along, and no one spoke ; they were all in communion of feeling with Jack, and hardly dared to move. The roar of the river with its monotonous whirl, the stars creeping out on the sky, the darkness without, the darkness within—and so they waited.

At last a shrill whistle broke on their ears, and a sudden swishing sound through the air, followed by a dull thud. Something had fallen, and they flew to the spot. Freddy's eyes were the first to make the discovery. A stone at the end of a length of reim, with a paper tied on to it.

He handed it to Jack, with a muttered 'Cheer up, old fellow !'

'Read it,' said Jack. 'I cannot.'

With Robin striking matches in his hat at his side, Freddy slowly puzzled out the pencil-scrawl on a morsel of soiled paper :

'Slight hope. *Believe* there is life, but don't *know* it. Am taking her home to do best. Listen for my gun to-night. Three shots the signal if she lives. If you hear two only, understand the *worst*.

'Uninjured, except by water.

'R. D.'

The last match fizzed out. The listening Kafirs drew away, making comments among themselves. Freddy pulled his hat over his eyes, and looked on the ground. At last Jack spoke quietly.

' I must hope,' he said.

' Yes, it is all you can do,' answered Robin ; ' and it might be worse. There is room for hope.'

' Try to keep even,' entreated Paulett. ' Don't make sure either way. I should judge it will be two hours before you can hear, at earliest.'

' I shall stay here,' said Jack firmly ; ' and, if you do not mind, I would rather be alone. I can bear it better. I shall watch —it may come any minute.'

They did not contradict him ; only they wrung his hand when they left him, and wished him God-speed! He climbed along the bank until he reached a big mimosa-tree, and under its shade he sat down, with his back resting against the trunk. There he might rest and listen for that crack of doom!

Looking at the quiet scene below him now, it was difficult to realize that the game of life and death had been played out there in such an awful manner. Jack's thoughts travelled compassionately to the man who had won and lost in one throw on that eventful day. He could think of him compassionately now, and in the egotism of our minds we are apt to pity the dead ; but he knew within himself that if the fiat went forth that night for Dollie, he would need more pity than the man who had left them.

The stars were sparkling in the sky now, and the clouds slowly drifting away to the westward ; the wind had fallen, and, but for that dull roll of the river below, the rest of the night brooded over everything.

The peace over the earth soothed him unconsciously, and he began somehow to hope. How much he had to be thankful for already, he thought, his eyes wandering to where Dare had performed his perilous feat ; it seemed to him like a promise. If he could only wrest that great gift of life by supplication, or by sacrifice, from the mighty

powers that be, how fair might be the
future! He should have no right to ask to
be blessed again; that boon in its immensity
might well ransom all future benefits that
Destiny might hold in store for him. 'Give
this only, and I will crave nothing more for
ever.' Ah, in our finite wisdom, our feeble
souls are apt to importune the Deity after
that manner!

'I should positively not have a thing
left to wish for,' mused Jack, his thoughts
precipitating themselves into the future;
and somehow, on this, back to his mind
came some words of Mrs. Dare's, 'Those
who have not—the gods take,' when he
had asked her if her happy face belied her;
and he shivered, as we shiver, they say,
when people are walking over our grave
that is to be. And then he woke up to
the fact that he was cold and exhausted,
and that a man cannot strike along the
scale of almost every human emotion within
a few hours, without paying for it—

physically. So he was glad when he heard
a voice say close to his ear :

'Baas, I have brought you some brandy.
Baas, Freddy send.' It was startlingly
close in the darkness, and Jack jumped
slightly, seeing which the man added, 'I
called to Baas, but he did not answer.'

Then a flask and a tin of biscuits were
put down beside him.

The moon was slowly rising, but the
light was yet indistinct, and Jack struck
a match to look at his watch—one hour
gone !

'Tell Mr. Freddy——' he began. Then
the match went hissing far into the water
below, and he jumped to his feet. 'Good
heavens! you here! you bird of ill-omen!
Why do you come to me *now* ?'

The sight of a face that had turned up
in the nick of time once before to destroy
his happiness, struck him with an ex-
aggerated sense of evil import.

September the Hottentot stepped back

at this address, while a snake-like sneer
curled his lips round his yellow teeth.

'My Baas has been killed to-day. I
stay by him. Klaas go to his supper—
asked me to bring the brandy. I thought
I should like to see Baas Jack again ; I
never forget Baas Jack. I look here—and
then I mind him.' And the Hottentot
showed, through his open shirt, the broad
scars the sjambock had left, earnestly
watching Jack's face the while.

If he expected any commiseration, he
had come at the wrong time to seek it.

'Right enough,' replied Jack carelessly.
'And if you do not clear off my place
before to-morrow morning, you may have
something else to remember me by.'

'Nie ! Baas Jack will flog me no more,'
said the Hottentot, with a dark frown. 'It
is right enough, is it ? So the great God
think, for He is white too. I loved my
Baas and I served him, and he is " dod."
And Baas Jack is—*alive*. Where I go,

Baas, if I not stay here?' with a sudden change of tone.

'Go to the devil, if you like—but get out of my sight, or I will throw you over those cliffs!'

'Ha!' said September. 'Baas Jack drove me out of my house, because he say I should not steal—I suppose Baas Jack is never hungry. Then he want to kill me, now he drive me away again. I go, and not let him kill me.'

'Don't stop here, making yourself out a black angel,' said Jack impatiently, with almost a grim smile. 'It is waste of your valuable time. I'll have none of your brood here. You are the most rascally set of Hottentots in the valley. As for you, you have always been up to some devilry since you were that high ; but I have cured you of taking me for buck, I fancy, and you will play your tricks elsewhere — you imp of Satan ! So, go !'

'Yah, I go,' said the Hottentot, taking up

his gun. Then with a slow grin he added :
' Baas Jack watch for Missie. I wish him
luck, as the white man say.'

The fiendish chuckle that followed the
words irritated Jack into fury; but as the
Hottentot had already moved away, he
choked it down as best he might.

' The yellow viper !' he muttered. ' I
would not have had a sight of him just now
for a thousand pounds. 'Twas a pity I let
him slip through my fingers after all that
day—I am tempted to think. He will only
go potting at some one else, some day—for
a nigger to find he can do anything with
impunity is dangerous—but I guess it won't
be me. No, that was a tidy thonging, upon
my word ! But when I remember that if
he had been strangled when he was born,
this night would not have been, I wonder—
well, I wonder I took him as I did to-night.
If a fellow is not answerable for all his evil
deeds, he certainly is not for some of his
good ones,' concluded Jack, with a sigh.

And then he drank some brandy, and took Dollie's picture out of his pocket, and looked at it in the light of the rising moon, to dismiss the thoughts that had ruffled him.

September went away down the river with evil and malice in his mind, and his yellow wrinkled face working ominously. He had come intending to sit out for buck in the moonlight, and because he, too, took his own interest in that question of life or death. His receding forehead crinkled itself into flatter lines than usual, and he twitched impatiently at his clothes, as he thought of how everything had gone wrong with him on that day, that had opened so fairly according to his views. Certainly he might have been drowned, but if he had been he would have gone to heaven, and turned white, and been as good as Baas Jack or any other man ; so the question of loss or gain on that point was a doubtful one. But he *had* lost a good master, and the revenge in which

39—2

his impish soul had taken delight. Baas Muller had repaid *his* score when he had married Missie, and now that was all swept away; and Baas Jack, the man who had hunted him and tried to kill him, might yet be happy, and he was powerless to stop it.

'Ah, but Missie will die—she looked dead,' he said to himself comfortingly. 'Then I shall not care, for Baas Jack will wish he was dead, and he will keep the mark of Missie all his days perhaps, as I shall keep the mark of his sjambock. Curse Baas Jack!' And the Hottentot doubled his fists, and wrinkled his face as he looked up at the stars. 'Yes, Missie *must* die!' he said, as he crept into a bush to lie in wait. 'Then I will take one look at Baas Jack's face, and go—to my people!'

A second hour had drifted slowly into the past; the moon had travelled up into the heavens, and the trees and rocks seemed to quiver in her intense light, and the river looked like one solid sheet of silver. But the silence had been unbroken save by the ordinary noises of the hour, and those two men still watched on in that solitude, one for life, and the other for death.

Jack had looked during a long time at Dollie's picture, until he had almost succeeded in dreaming himself into the paradise he desired, with that face on his breast for life. But as he felt that the ordeal must be drawing nigh, he closed the case and put it back on his heart, much as he might have done with a charm. How he dreaded while he longed for the sound of a gun! Perhaps human nature, even in youth, is at bottom pessimist; in age it is natural it should be so, and the man who is brought up in a wild country, and lives from his cradle in the atmosphere of danger and self-dependence, is in heart older, although simpler, than the European product of the same age.

Jack's restlessness by-and-by attacked his legs, and he paced up and down, until, feeling as if the sound even of his own footfalls might distract his ears, he threw himself down on the rocks, where he could gaze up into that illimitable vault overhead, and speculate whether *she* could have passed away thither without his feeling it, and ponder on some mysteries that did not often bother Jack's matter-of-fact brain.

As the time still slipped on, he took it as an ill-omen, while he remembered the Hottentot's sudden appearance, and anguish and dull fear began to take possession of him, and he set his teeth and almost groaned aloud in the visions he conjured up for himself.

For the first time in his life, perhaps, he felt absolutely powerless ; and it bewildered him, for he was used to self-dependence. Jack's faith was a simple and reverent one—he was not troubled with any subtleties of modern thought—but his creed in its simplicity was but an accentuated definition of the saying, ' Providence helps those who help themselves.' His life had

led him to that conclusion; and it was
strange to him to stand aside simply as an
onlooker, and act neither as the instrument
nor the controller of fate.   Still Jack's be-
liefs on all points were absolute, or non-
existent, so that life was not the puzzle to
him that it is to some people.

Did he pray as the moments passed, bearing away hope in their flight ?   Were those
wild words prayers ?   He did not know.
He only felt, as he lay there under those
starry legions, that there was a Great Power
throbbing through the universe, and he
turned to it in his helplessness with the
faith that is childlike.

Away in the bush the Hottentot sat purring out *his* happiness at the delay, for he,
too, guessed its sinister meaning ; and from
time to time he took furtive notice of Jack's
movements, while he crooned to himself,
' Missie is *dead*—Missie is *dead.*'

' Two hours and a half !' exclaimed Jack,
pulling out his watch.   But the watch

suddenly slipped through his fingers, as he sprang to his feet and stood erect in the moonlight, the sense of hearing strained to the uttermost. Yes, it was no mistake, for distant, but sufficiently distinct, like a sudden stroke on the air, fell that sound of firing :

Boom !

And Jack stood steady now—the real time for endurance had come; but all his life seemed to have passed into his ears.

September, too, had crouched eagerly forward and clasped his gun closely and unconsciously, and his lips looked as if they had rolled back from his teeth, and stiffened so.

Boom ! It had come at last, with sixty seconds between. And now the springs of life seemed arrested, momentarily, for both those watchers.

Sixty other seconds elapsed, and it was still blank. In the delirium of his joy, September sprang from his lair. He could not curb his desire to look at Jack. He saw him standing there with one hand clenched over his heart, his face rigid, his eyes strained wide open. It was the paralysis of despair setting in.

' Ha!' whispered the Hottentot, laying his hand over his scarred chest, and rolling his eyes to heaven. ' Me smart no more.'

The silence lasted, while Jack stood there mute and motionless, and an onlooker might well have believed that with him the mechanism of life had suddenly run down.

Boom!

Louder and heavier than the preceding ones, the report which was to make the magic three rolled out on the air, as if it had only taken that pause to gather to itself fresh strength. Like an electric shock it roused Jack.

He threw up his hands with a gesture of exultation, and a joyous smile lit up his features. He was a living, breathing, human being again, whose life lay fair before him.

From out the dark night of suffering he had passed at a breath into the bright day-dawn. It had broken for him as it breaks on all our lives some day, and we look back over the long thorny way and it seems but a span. The Hottentot, with a snarl like a mad dog, clenched his teeth on his arm. ' Missie lives ! *Damn* Baas Jack !' The warm blood flowed over his lips, and fired him like wine.

' *Damn* Baas Jack !' he cried again, as he lifted his head. A ray of moonlight glinted on his figure, and Jack saw him suddenly. But he was beyond the influence of omens now.

' Bah ! that snake is scotched this time,' he muttered. And that radiant flashing smile broke over his face again.

' Damn Baas Jack !' reiterated the Hottentot the third time, with deadly meaning, as he seized his gun.

But Jack dreamed blindly on. Then, without warning to reach him in his joy,

the bolt sped. Treachery and murder
marked him down ; and, like a tree riven
by lightning, he fell with a sudden headlong crash to the ground. The earth and
sky danced together before his eyes as they
closed in darkness, and a fourth report,
sounding in its sullenness like a death-knell,
was the last conscious sound on his ears.

But Dollie's picture rested on his heart,
and that careful aim had been taken in vain,
for the murderous bullet turned aside and
sped on its course.

He was breathless and stunned. It was
insensibility, complete and instant, but it
passed quickly. Dazed, he found himself
wondering, while his eyes were still closed,
whether he was really dead or not, and
whether he should open them again on this
world, or haply on a new one. Jack lay
still for a moment; then he slowly raised
his eyelids, with that wonder as to what he
should see, his dominant thought.

No, it was not *Heaven* certainly—it might
be *Hell!* A dark, hideous face, with greed
of death for him in its eyes, was bending
down over him. While he looked it was
suddenly averted with a cry of despair, like
the disappointed howl of a wild beast ; and
a gun-stock gleamed in the air over his
head.

Memory of events came rushing back on
him in a strong clear flood.

No, it was *not* Hell. It was *life*. And
life that must be fought for instantly, or lost!

He caught that uplifted arm between his
fingers, and, as if by a lever, dragged himself up by it; and once on his feet, he knew
that he was unhurt.

One moment he held on with an iron
grip to the limb, while everything whirled
before him ; and then his arms were flung
round that yellow shrunken figure, and
together the two men swayed, while each
step carried them nearer and nearer the
bank.

The Hottentot twined himself like a snake round the Englishman's athletic limbs, but to no purpose. He was fighting for his life, and he tore and bit and snarled like the wild dog he was, but all in vain.

For a few moments the hideous struggle lasted, while the white moon looked calmly down on the raging human passions ; then it ended, as it was always bound to end— Jack's muscular fingers round the Hottentot's throat, his quivering form in his grasp, held high over the river that should receive it.

'Too good a grave for carrion !' cried Jack, as his grasp relaxed.

What thought had struck him?

For he clutched the Hottentot closely again with his strong hands, and lifting his arms high, flung the man away into a bush behind him.

He stood looking over the river, while his pulses thumped slowly into their regular course again, and his eyes were seeking vainly for what had arrested their glance a moment before.

Jack, when he spoke of it afterwards, always maintained that for one instant, on that moonlit road across the river, he had seen Dollie's figure distinctly as the fight ended.

It may have been a result of bodily exhaustion, an illusion generated by the brain so fearfully stamped with that one personality during so many hours; it probably was, unless she, hovering on the borderland between life and death, had power to appear to the man she loved. The links are almost loosened—the spirit is free to wander! Such things have been vouched for, until we can only turn aside and say that we have no *proof* of its being impossible. But no explanation could shake Jack's conviction that he had seen Dollie, and that through her came the thought which stayed his hand.

Ah, we all have our good angels visit us in one form or another!

The Hottentot sat there blinking, where Jack had flung him. His yellow face was puckered up, and his breath came in sobs. He was a sickly-looking sight with that fear of death so lately before his eyes. Presently he dragged himself painfully out of the bush, and crouched lower and lower, moving towards Jack as a whipped hound does.

Jack stood beyond with Dollie's picture in his hand, dreaming of the unshadowed joy that was dawning for him in the near future; but he heard the movement, and turned to watch the man—on his guard. Was he going to fly at his throat under this mask?

'Back!' he cried. 'Don't come near me, you vermin! You have had mercy, not justice, this time; and I cannot take God to witness for such as you; but, I do swear by the devil that owns you, that the next time you tempt me to kill you, I will *do it!* Now—go!'

But the Hottentot crouched on.

Suddenly he threw himself forward with a rapid movement, his body writhing on the ground, and wildly kissed Jack's feet, and sobbed the while. Then, clasping his hands together, he looked up supplicatingly at the man who had stayed his hand and given him back the life which he had forfeited, and such truth and fidelity as his black soul knew prompted the eager broken words that fell from his lips :

'Baas is *good*. September will die for Baas some day. Let him stay by him always.'

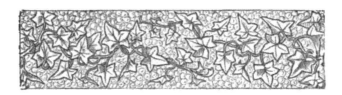

CHAPTER XV.

THE DAWN IS BREAKING.

MR. CRAIG stood at his front door. Jack leaned against the veranda opposite to him, with his hands in his pockets. They had had a long business interview that morning.

'Well, my boy,' said Mr. Craig at last, taking a deep breath, 'you will make your bed, and you will lie on it, and you will not be singular in that. And you will wish to unmake it some day, or you will be very singular indeed. In the front of such a calamity as your marrying, I'm bound to hope for the best and fear the worst—as you must with women. There is your mother, for instance, a good woman as they go nowadays, as I have always said. For she has not dragged me into the Divorce Court, nor schemed to poison me, nor yet spent any of my pennies she could not lay her fingers on! And when she goes further, and don't present you with any more of her sort—knowing your objection to them—she is more than that; she is a woman of good taste! But you see, Jack, you cannot hope for these advantages in a wife—though they are but negative after all—because, for one reason, I did not choose your mother—I beg her pardon, let her choose me—until my wisdom-teeth were well grown, and I connot help thinking that in your case you might have *gone farther and fared better.* A man should keep up to his mark in women, as in other things; it avoids perplexity for him. However, you will have grief enough, my boy, so let us be merry while we can. The girl is pretty, certainly. Well! You would not be your father's son and go and choose an ugly woman—we don't take any other blots of creation and stick them in our houses; and—yes, she is a nice little girl. And then there is the solid part—the guineas——'

' Oh, hang the money !'

' To be sure, to be sure! We couldn't get along without that. That is the symptom of your complaint, and a *very* singular one it is. Ah, Jack! you look like a fool to-day, and you speak like a fool ; and it is borne in upon me more strongly than usual that you ought to have married a clever woman to keep you straight, instead of looking out a bigger fool than yourself. It is hard on the next generation, 'pon my soul it is !'

Jack laughed. His radiant good-humour was proof against any such attacks, and the old mirth echoed in his laugh.

' Well, sir, you will have Freddy yet——'

' Eh !' grumbled Mr. Craig. ' I fancy

40—2

your mother was about to invite the Governor's daughters here for your benefit; now she will have to take up with Freddy instead. You are like your mother, Jack —that's where it is! A great mistake for a man to be like his mother; it gives him a heart, and makes a fool of him. Well, Freddy, I flatter myself, takes after *me;* and you will not find him marrying for love, and sentimental rubbish——'

'John dear!' remonstrated Mrs. Craig plaintively from her chair in the dining-room. 'You do say such *odd* things.'

'Hum!' growled Mr. Craig. 'Didn't know you were there, my dear. This marriage puts everything out of my head. I did hope *our* example—— Ah well, never mind!'

'The gov's bark is worse than his bite,' said Jack musingly, watching his father progressing along the veranda, slowly shaking his head. 'He was generous and kindly beyond what I expected this morning, though I thought I knew his measure pretty well by this time.'

'As for *me*,' interposed Freddy loftily, strolling out of a clump of custard-apple trees in the garden, ' don't go speculating on me! For I shall *never* marry. The governor chose to do it and stick me here —I couldn't help that! But I'm hanged if I am going to hand on the burden of sin and misery and broiling *I* enjoy, to any poor devil! Another thing is that I think a tarnation lot of myself, if no one else does ; and I am never likely to see the woman who comes up to *my* mark. If I did, I suppose she wouldn't look at me.'

' She might look over your head, I'm afraid, Freddy.'

'Great men are always undersized : Napoleon, Nelson, Wellington, heaps of 'em. You cannot have body and brains too. Why, there you are to prove it!'

'I don't think I am quite so bad as that comes to,' said Jack reflectively.

'No,' returned Freddy; 'between ourselves, I think you are uncommon 'cute—
but that ain't brains. Ta, ta; this kind of
orange-blossom-and-cake conversation is
not to my taste. I *am* like the governor—
no mistake about it!'

'I hope he will stick to it,' growled Mr.
Craig, as he lighted his pipe at the end of
the veranda. 'But men have been craving
after women, and cursing 'em afterwards,
ever since Adam first started the kind of
thing, and I have *no faith* in him!'

'Never mind, dear,' said Mrs. Craig,
jumping up from her chair and linking her
arm affectionately in her eldest son's. 'I
will love her, if no one else does. Of course
she will have a husband to be proud of,
but I was always proud of your father;
and I *believe* in love, Jack—it will wear
through so much. If she makes you happy,
I will be content. You would be miserable
married without love, for you *have* a warm,
loving nature, my son. Ah, your father

said that; but he forgot to say, what no
one knows better, how it endears you to us
all, and makes " Jack " a favourite far and
wide.' .

'My dear mother, you are trying to
smooth my ruffled feathers with a ven-
geance! But if you will be kind to Dollie,
it will gladden that heart—*I ought not to
have had!* And Jack bent down and
kissed the mother who had been such a
loving counsellor and friend to him always,
and added gravely, 'I shall be a lucky
fellow indeed if my wife turns out the prize
my little mother has been to me.'

'Bless you, dear!' responded Mrs. Craig
tenderly, looking up at her son with misty
eyes. 'I don't blame Dolly at all. How
could she *help* loving you, if she tried!'

And then the horses came round to take
Robin and Jack up to the Dares'.

It was the first day on which the river
had been properly fordable, although the
Kafirs had swum across once or twice

during the week with tidings of Dollie's progress.

'He is coming, dear,' said Mrs. Dare softly, bending over the couch where Dollie lay wrapped in a long blue dressing-gown.

Very delicate and frail she looked, but what a happy little face it was! She gave a slight sigh, but it was of joy, not sorrow; then the colour flushed into her face, as she threw her arms suddenly round Mrs. Dare's neck.

'I wish I was beautiful and clever like you,' she said wistfully; 'then I might hope he would love me always, as he does now. You would keep him, but I am not fit to be his wife. He will find it out some day, and then—I shall break my heart.'

'You are a-fishin'!' answered Mrs. Dare gaily. 'And I will not gratify you by bringing you the looking-glass.' Then, seeing the earnest look on the little innocent face that had grown dear to her through hours of watching over the flickering life, she added, with sweet gravity, 'Don't be afraid. You have won him to yourself from all other women ; surely, you may guard his love by the same charms. Be to him always, as much as is possible, what you were when he wooed you, and then you will keep him, for he is worth keeping. I think, Dollie, if women would try more to do this, fewer marriages would be unhappy. We talk of men changing after, but I fancy sometimes it is not their fault alone. Perhaps,' added Mrs. Dare brightly, ' some men recognise our identity after the honeymoon as little as we do theirs. Now I will make you spick-and-span.'

Rockingham Dare went out to meet and welcome his visitors as soon as the sound of galloping horses reached his ears. As it was their first meeting since that eventful night, there was a great deal to be said on both sides. Dare, with his left arm in a sling, looked a very hero in their eyes.

The meeting was a rather silent one at first, as meetings are apt to be when deep feelings are called to the surface.   Jack attempted to express his undying sense of obligation, which he felt in himself no words could adequately convey, and Rockingham Dare was equally resolute to hear nothing about it.   He dismissed the subject characteristically.

'I want no thanks, Jack, for what was but an act of common humanity.   And if I did, the sight of your face—which is a pictur' this day—would give me all I need in that direction.'

This was turning the tables indeed, and Jack had to confess himself beaten, and allow the conversation to flow into other channels.   Presently Dare invited him to go on to the house, and he went along the veranda alone.

Mrs. Dare stood in the doorway, and held out her hand to him with heartfelt welcome. As her heart had ached for him in his long days of sorrow, so sincerely did she now rejoice with him.

' A thousand welcomes to-day, Jack, and —God bless you both !' she said earnestly, with her brightest smile.

Jack took her hand. She had long been his ideal woman, and now she had tenderly nursed the girl he loved back to life. He did not feel that he could say much, but he *did* say hurriedly, as he raised her white hand to his lips :

' I think you are an angel, not a woman !'

' Ah, no,' she said ; ' the " angel " is else- where. Come and see her.'

She threw open the door of an inner room, and those two who had suffered so hardly for one another were face to face, with no barrier between them, at last—and their eyes met. A look of yearning love on the girl's part, of eager, bounding joy, unshadowed, on the man's, and then he had gathered her into his arms, her head rested on his breast. The queen had won her king!

Mrs. Dare softly closed the door.

Robin and Dare sat on the veranda, where she joined them, and they passed an hour in pleasant chat. It was Robin's farewell visit to them.

'Mr. Bordingley came on Sunday,' remarked Mrs. Dare. 'Of course, I was too busy and anxious to be able to see much of him, but Rock was delighted with him. I don't know whether the slow dreary gravity with which he recounts his misfortunes, or his sudden bursts of cheerfulness, are most laughable? You should have heard his melancholy greeting to me on Sunday.'

'Ah, I have come at the wrong time, Mrs. Dare. Well, if I could not have studied it out to come at the wrong time, naturally I should not have come at all.'

'I am glad you unearthed him—he is a treasure,' returned Dare. 'I have often asked him, but I fancy he seldom goes anywhere.'

' Well, we must not lose sight of him now,' said Mrs. Dare. ' I quite shiver to think of him, living in that hole.'

' Hole !' exclaimed Dare. ' Bordingley's is a fine place. Best soil round.'

' *Soil !*' ejaculated Mrs. Dare scornfully. ' You cannot talk to soil.'

Robin and Dare smiled.

' Ah, I never notice that men talk less than women when they are together,' said Mrs. Dare, with deep gravity. ' And I am sure they are quite as inquisitive and curious about their neighbours as we are, " under the rose." Is not a man really delighted if you collect news for him, and is he not eager and anxious if he thinks you are keeping anything back ? Of course, when he has extracted it all, he will say there is nothing he " despises like gossip ;" but we know how much *that* is worth ! Now poor Mr. Bordingley has an enforced dearth of all these things, and many more necessary.'

' What a sketch of a wasted life!' returned Robin solemnly, as they all went in to tea, and Jack put in an appearance again, wearing a jubilant sunshiny expression on his face, that everyone tried hard to appear unconscious of.

' Sit in *your* chair,' said Mrs. Dare. ' You are the hero of the day, certainly. I will pour out some tea for Dollie presently, which perhaps you would like to take in.'

Jack settled himself comfortably in the chair.

' There is no one to dispute this seat of honour with me to-day. Poor old Seymour!' A shade passed over Mrs. Dare's bright face. ' An odd fish!' continued Jack. ' I said so the day he came, and again when he went. But I believe he is a rattling good fellow for all that.'

' Sure to be, in your present frame of

mind,' suggested Robin. 'I should think even September the Hottentot is a rattling good fellow to-day.'

Jack laughed.

'I don't know,' he said. 'He has a rather worse taste in my mouth than most people.'

'I prophesy great things for old Seymour in the future. Did you not hear from him to-day?' asked Robin.

'Yes, so I did. Glad you reminded me. I am making a collection of all our photos for him. He said when he left he should like some specimens of the "natives" to astonish the folks at home—and, will you add yours, Mrs. Dare? You see, it will raise the reputation of the "gallery" no end. Seymour told me to ask you—said you had promised it him long ago.'

'Photos are productive of a great deal of immorality in the way of perjury,' remarked Robin.

'I think I have his letter here,' said

Jack, diving in his pockets. 'Yes, here
it is :

' " Dear Jack,

' " Will you kindly send on my
traps first opportunity, as I sail next week?
—and *don't* forget the photos. I enclose
my home address. Will you write to me ?
I should like to know how you all go on ;
Freddy specially, and "—there is a blot or a
smudge here—" the colony.

' " Yours in haste,

' " Lucas Seymour."

Odd fish.'

'The colony ! What did you reply ?'
asked Robin, with a face impassive as a
sphinx.

'Why—I said, just this. Letters are not
my strong point :

' " Dear Seymour,

' " Your traps and photos are going
down with Adair, who starts to-morrow.

I will write when there is anything to tell about Freddy; and as to the colony, let me recommend you the *Argus*—it is a good un for news. I will send it if you like. We have missed you uncommon, considerin'.

' " Yours,

' " JACK." '

' If brevity is the soul of wit, those two should be framed,' remarked Dare gravely.

Mrs. Dare had been looking into the tea-pot with a rather serious face, but now she looked up with a smile.

' Oh, Jack ! what would you do if you had to write love-letters ?'

' I should never get married. Never a woman would have me,' responded Jack, pondering the subject.

Then Robin went in with Jack to take leave of Dollie, and Mrs. Dare went thoughtfully to her writing-table, and took a photo out of the drawer.

It was her last communication probably with Lucas Seymour in this world, and she felt a solemnity about it. How truly he had loved her! and how often his face of haggard yet self-controlled misery in that moment of parting was before her eyes! She knew intuitively that the bloom was off his life for awhile—who could say for how long? He might be an odd fish, but she had grown to like him; and he had given her that rare and perfect love which is not of the earth, earthy—whose very breath is self-sacrifice. A bright jewel in the crown of womanhood to her who wins it, though it may chance that through all time she may be unable or un- willing to wear it. She remembered his last request, and, with a throb of compassion, dipped her pen in the ink. To compassion- ate all forms of suffering was as natural to her as to breathe. Across the photo, at the back, she wrote, 'To my friend.' Then she dropped it into an envelope and fastened it.

Perhaps those three words might be a

sheet-anchor some day, when life, as he had said, ' got a bit hard.'

When Jack came out she handed it to him. And then Robin said anxiously :

' I have been trying to persuade Jack not to put off his marriage long. What do you say, Mrs. Dare ?'

Their eyes met for an instant.

' I agree with you,' she returned, with a sad look in hers. ' And the circumstances are peculiar. I think they need not much consider formalities.'

' Dollie is hardly recovered yet. It must take time. Such a shock and chill would try a man, let alone a delicate woman,' replied Jack.

' Of course,' said Robin. ' I only said, don't dawdle for ever, Cape-fashion. Make hay while the sun shines ! I have so little hay of my own, that I take interest in other people's.'

' You cannot very well take more interest in that hay than I do,' responded Jack,

41—2

laughing. 'Drink our healths when you land—I dare say you will be about to date. Are you horrified, Mrs. Dare?'

'No,' she replied slowly. 'You seem to have belonged to one another so long.'

When Jack had gone out, Robin turned to Mrs. Dare:

'Miss Dollie—by-the-bye, I suppose she is *not* Miss Dollie——'

'Oh, we all call her so,' put in Mrs. Dare hastily. 'It hardly seemed like a marriage.'

'Well, Miss Dollie is very lovely—more so than I had ever thought her. *That* kind of beauty——'

'Ah, don't!' said Mrs. Dare, shrinking back. 'I will put no obstacles in their way, nor let anyone else, and—it may come right.'

'Yes—yes, it *may*. But stand to your decision. And now I must say good-bye to another of my kind friends. If I were not going to settle down into a virtuous stay-at-home married man, I might hope in some of my wanderings to come across you again, but now the chances are remote.'

'Who can tell? The world is small,' replied Mrs. Dare. 'We shall miss you very much, and hope for your happiness, wherever you may be.'

'Thanks. I have had some happy days with the Craigs, who are truly kind people; and it will be long before I forget Craigmount—also the fair lady who is the veriest incarnation of a sunbeam I ever met. They will know at home that I come from the country of the diamond,' added Robin, smiling; 'but I shall be able to tell them of a pearl that Africa could ill spare. Such a perfect lustrous jewel that a king might be proud to place it in his crown!'

'Ah, you mean me!' said Mrs. Dare, with a sudden bright laugh, reading Robin's face; 'but that pretty description does not apply to me in the least.'

'*Could* it apply to anyone else?'

'You are very kind, but too sadly flattering.   People *are* always kind to me—I don't know how it is,' said Mrs. Dare musingly. ' When I hear people say the world is not a pleasant place, I often wonder at it.'

' The world, O fair philosopher, is pleasant to those who are pleasant unto it. Adieu!'

Mrs. Dare leaned over the veranda-trellis with her husband, and listened to the sound of the retreating horses' feet.

' There goes the last of my old photos,' she said, laughing.   ' They were my favourites.'

' Hum! Did you think to send Seymour *mine?'*

' No; it did not occur to me,' replied Mrs. Dare, after an imperceptible pause.

' That's a pity.   He will be disappointed.'

Mrs. Dare looked up quickly.   How much did he know or guess ?

Rockingham Dare answered the look with a smile.

' No,' he said, ' I have never yet wished

my wife of a " discreet plainness," though people have the bad taste to prefer her photos to mine.'

Mrs. Dare passed over the remark in silence, and looked somewhat wistfully away over the veldt.

' All going,' she said, ' one after another, to the dear old country. We shall miss Mr. Adair, he was so pleasant ; and I suppose we shall never see any of them again.'

Dare smiled mischievously.

' I don't know about Adair ; but if some of those elephants and buffaloes you fancy were to make an end of me some day, I think you might see Seymour again, anyway.'

' Rock,' said Mrs. Dare suddenly, linking her arm round his, and looking up with those glorious eyes. ' Doesn't he know, doesn't everyone know, that if anything happened to you, I should just lie down on your grave—and *stay there ?*'

' I could not have a more beautiful blossom there,' returned Rock Dare very tenderly. 'But I am not so selfish that, if I could no longer take care of her myself, I would not rather my flower grew on an honest man's breast than on my grave.'

She laid her soft cheek against his, while her great eyes grew dewy with feeling.

'Never, darling!' she answered, in the low sweet voice that was music to his ears. Then, glancing up at the far-stretching blue sky, she added softly, 'We know not how, *but love shall be with us for ever there.*'

CHAPTER XVI.

SUNLIGHT.

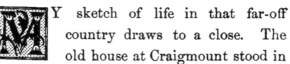Y sketch of life in that far-off country draws to a close. The old house at Craigmount stood in the full sunlight of an early December morning. The veranda was ablaze with blossom, and the scent of the tropical flowers hung heavy on the air. The stoop was littered with bags, and portmanteaus, and karosses, and odds and ends of luggage. Jack and Robin stood amongst it, looking out.

'Yes, that is Klaas,' said the former, dropping a telescope with which he had been surveying the veldt. 'The English mail is in, then. You will be able to get your letters before you start.'

' Just as well, but I don't suppose there will be anything of any consequence,' replied Robin.

In a few minutes the boy galloped up to the stoop, and the post-bag was in their hands.

' Now I wonder whether they were worth waiting for ?' muttered Robin, as Jack handed him two, and then went into the house with the bag to distribute the rest. He tore the first open, and read it quickly; then folded it back, and read it again slowly. It ran thus :

' LINCOLN'S INN FIELDS.

' *November* —, 1880.

' DEAR SIR,

' We are exceedingly sorry to inform you that Desmond and Co. have stopped payment. We fear your loss will be very considerable, and, what is yet more embarrassing, Mr. Peters, who holds the last mortgage on Holm Lea, being deeply in-

volved with the bank, has given notice that
he must foreclose without delay. There is
no amount of interest due, for, as you are
aware, it has been paid up since you came
into the property. But to provide this
large sum at such short notice, in view of
the serious defalcations resulting from the
bank failure, is a matter of great difficulty.
We are, however, making arrangements to
meet that difficulty, while waiting instructions from you, as we conclude that it is
not your wish to let Holm Lea go into the
market. We would suggest that the place
might be let for a few years, to meet the
reduction in income; and that, as you have
lived so much abroad, you might not be dis-
inclined to go on doing so, and to retrench.
The Australian property is rising in value.
We should be glad to learn your wishes at
the earliest opportunity, and to do our
utmost to meet them. Having conducted
your family business for so many years, we
cannot conclude without assurances of our

sincere regret for this most unexpected calamity.

> 'We remain, dear sir,
>> 'Yours truly,
>>> 'FOGGETT AND DAWSON.'

'Humph!' said Robin at last, twirling the letter round his fingers. 'I suppose this is beastly serious. Who'd have thought it of Desmond? Poor Holm Lea! I believe there is a curse over the old place—or, perhaps, it is over me. It held well enough together in my father's lifetime, who really went the pace; and now, when I have tried to clear off mortgages, this is the result! It is not lucky to take up a mortgage, I conclude.

He looked over the letter again, then folded it up with a shrug of the shoulders.

'Retrench!' he exclaimed scornfully. 'Have I ever done otherwise, since I came into the property? Perhaps I had better go and live in Australia. My marriage will be off, of course.'

He paced up and down the veranda in deep thought. It seemed to him that his six-and-thirty years were beginning to tell on him. He felt old and weary.

' Ah, well,' he said at last. ' I shall not be a beggar. And I have no children to leave the old place to. I dare say it is all for the best. I am sure I was meant for single blessedness until I meet Mary in another world—if there is another. Trust it is not after the pattern of this one.'

He crushed the letter back into his pocket, and, as he did so, drew out another.

' I had forgotten this one—something else pleasant, I suppose. Such delights usually hunt in couples.' He slowly broke it open.

'—— HALL, HAMPSHIRE.
' *November* —, 1880.
' MY DEAREST ROBIN,

' I am limited to a shabby line, lest I should lose the mail. What a dear old boy you were to send all those beautiful feathers ! The children and I are delighted with our treasures. I should indeed like to see an ostrich, a " full-feather bird." *Do* you think you could get one stuffed as a curiosity for us, as you say they die sometimes? I fancy it would look nice in the hall with Donald's " Bengalee," and perhaps other people might not have one. I enclose you a cutting from the *Times* that Donald has just brought to my room. Of course, it is very sad, and I feel very much for Mary, though no one could think she had a great deal to regret; but there is some one even nearer to my heart than poor Mary, whose wandering life all these years has been such a sore grief to me.

' My beloved brother, don't be angry with me, but a little bird seems to tell me that I shall see you in England now before long. With love from us both, and a hug from little Robin,

' Always your loving
' SISTER.

' Write to me *at once.*'

'Jack!' called Robin at length, in deep tones; 'Jack!'

'Hey?' said Jack, coming out from the house. 'Is it the cart?'

'Read those two letters,' said Robin simply.

As if lost in a dream, he sat on the bench while Jack did as he was bid.

'Well,' said Jack at last, looking up with a half-smile, 'am I to condole or congratulate? I am ready to do either.'

Robin took them from his hand, and rose from his seat.

'This one,' he said, pointing to the lawyers', 'will lose me money and *other things. This one*'—and his voice softened —'will win me the woman I love.' He looked up with a long sigh of happiness, while he drew himself up to his full height, as a man who casts off the burden of years. And his deep-toned voice faltered as he said slowly, 'Thank God! I shall dwell in the sunlight at last!'

And the Cape cart came round to take him the first stage on his journey.

*   *   *   *   *

Jack also passed into the sunlight; for in a month he brought home his fair little bride, and it seemed as if he had lived to gather in his harvest of happiness with both hands.

' My Dollie grows stronger and stronger every day,' Jack would say with pride, as he watched her blossom into more vivid beauty in the almost southern glow of his great love for her, and win all hearts by her simple, gentle ways.

Through that summer her big blue eyes grew more wonderfully dark and lustrous, and the lovely bloom on her cheeks deepened as the months rolled on. Then the summer slowly faded, and she faded with it, suddenly and softly as a leaf falls to the ground in autumn.

And the Kafirs point to her resting-place on the hillside, where the white flowers

always bloom, and the blue-gums cast l
shadows ; and will tell the passer-by
story of her wedding-eve, of her stra
rescue from a watery grave, and of how
dwelt among them by Jack's side in shad
less content.

Alas ! there is no Eden now in wl
mortals are permitted to dwell. So
envious Death-angel just brushed that
fect life with his wing, and she arose
followed him, looking back wistfully,
may be, until she had crossed the w
dark river.

Does not she, too, dwell in the sunlig

THE END.

BILLING AND SONS, PRINTERS, GUILDFORD.
S. & H.

CPSIA information can be obtained
at www.ICGtesting.com
Printed in the USA
BVHW040827241220
596434BV00014B/241

9 781166 475178